# Ethical Musicality

*Ethical Musicality* addresses the crossroads between music and ethics, combining philosophical knowledge, theoretical reflection, and practical understanding. When tied together, music and ethics link profoundly, offering real-life perspectives that would otherwise be inaccessible to us. The first part elucidates music and ethics through some influential and selected scholars ranging from Antiquity via modern philosophy to contemporary voices. In the second part, different roles and arenas are illustrated and explored through various music practices in real-life encounters for the musician, the music educator, the music therapist, the musicologist, the 'lay' musician, and the music researcher. The third part unfolds an *ethical musicality* focusing on the body, relationship, time, and space. Following these fundamental existentials, ethical musicality expands our lifeworld, including context, involvement, power, responsibility, sustainability, and hope. Such an ethical musicality meets us with a calling *to* humanity—offering hope of a 'good life'.

**Gro Trondalen** is Professor of Music Therapy at the Norwegian Academy of Music, Oslo, Norway.

# Music and Change: Ecological Perspectives

Series Editor:
Gary Ansdell
*Nordoff Robbins and University of Exeter*
Professor Tia DeNora
*Department of Sociology & Philosophy, HuSS
University of Exeter, UK*

Series advisory board:
Kenneth Aigen
*Temple University, USA*
Jane Davidson
*University of Western Australia*
Timothy Dowd
*Emory University, USA*
Lucy Green
*Institute of Education, UK*
Lee Higgins
*Boston University College of Fine Arts, USA*
Raymond MacDonald
*Edinburgh University, UK*
Mercédès Pavlicevic
*Nordoff Robbins, UK*
Even Ruud
*Norwegian Academy of Music, Norway*
Brynjulf Stige
*University of Bergen, Norway*
Henry Stobart
*Royal Holloway, University of London, UK*

*Music and Change: Ecological Perspectives*, is a cross-disciplinary, topic-led series for scholars and practitioners. Its aim is to explore the question of how, where and when music makes a difference. If music is a dynamic ingredient of change, what are the processes and mechanisms associated with music's powers, and how can ecological perspectives help us to understand music in action? Book proposals are welcome in any of the following areas: healthcare, social policy, political activism, psychiatry, embodiment, mind and consciousness, community relations, education and informal learning, management and organizational cultures, trauma, memory and commemoration, theories of action, self-help, conflict and conflict resolution, governance, resistance, protest, and utopian communities.

**Ethical Musicality**
*Gro Trondalen*

For more information about this series, please visit: www.routledge.com/music/series/MC

# Ethical Musicality

## Gro Trondalen

LONDON AND NEW YORK

First published 2023
by Routledge
4 Park Square, Milton Park, Abingdon, Oxon OX14 4RN

and by Routledge
605 Third Avenue, New York, NY 10158

*Routledge is an imprint of the Taylor & Francis Group, an informa business*

© 2023 Gro Trondalen

The right of Gro Trondalen to be identified as author of this work has been asserted in accordance with sections 77 and 78 of the Copyright, Designs and Patents Act 1988.

The Open Access version of this book, available at www.taylorfrancis.com, has been made available under a Creative Commons Attribution-Non Commercial-No Derivatives (CC-BY-NC-ND) 4.0 International license. Funded by Norwegian Academy of Music.

*Trademark notice*: Product or corporate names may be trademarks or registered trademarks, and are used only for identification and explanation without intent to infringe.

*British Library Cataloguing-in-Publication Data*
A catalogue record for this book is available from the British Library

*Library of Congress Cataloging-in-Publication Data*
Names: Trondalen, Gro, author.
Title: Ethical musicality/Gro Trondalen.
Description: First edition. | New York: Ashgate, 2023. | Series: Music and change: ecological perspectives | Includes bibliographical references and index.
Identifiers: LCCN 2022054267 | ISBN 9781032111261 (hardback) | ISBN 9781032111308 (paperback) | ISBN 9781003218524 (ebook)
Subjects: LCSH: Music-Moral and ethical aspects.
Classification: LCC ML3920 .T76 2023 | DDC 780/.017—dc23/eng/20221115
LC record available at https://lccn.loc.gov/2022054267

ISBN: 978-1-032-11126-1 (hbk)
ISBN: 978-1-032-11130-8 (pbk)
ISBN: 978-1-003-21852-4 (ebk)

DOI: 10.4324/9781003218524

Written with support from the Norwegian Non-fiction Writers and Translators Association and publication support from the Norwegian Academy of Music.

To
**Aurora, Ask, Olav, Nora, Marie**

# Contents

*Acknowledgements* viii

Introduction 1

1 Ethics as a discipline: a music-philosophical discourse 7

2 Ethics as a practice: music in real-life encounters 29

3 Reflexivity: music and ethics 59

*Index* 91

# Acknowledgements

Many people have contributed to shaping my music-and-ethics journey. I am inspired by innovative colleagues at the Norwegian Academy of Music, Centre for Research in Music and Health (CREMAH): Karette Stensæth (N), Felicity Baker (AU), Lars Ole Bonde (DK), and Even Ruud (N). Also, the music therapy training colleagues mean a lot to me. Thanks for your laughter and professional dedication. I am encouraged by you: the new generation of leaders, clinicians, teachers and researchers. The previous Head of the Department of Music Pedagogy and Music Therapy, Brit Ågot Brøske (N), supported the 'Ethical Reflection Supervision Training Program' at the right time. Thanks. Also, thanks to inspiring collaboration at the PhD program in music represented by Øivind Varkøy (N).

I am grateful for all I have learned from serving on Ethics Commissions at the national and international levels. A special thanks to Esperanza Torres (ES) and Hans Peter Weber (CH) for collaborative work at the Ethics Committee for the European Association for Guided Imagery and Music. Likewise, I am grateful for inspirational and collective work with colleagues worldwide within the Research and Ethics Commission for the World Federation of Music Therapy, represented by Amy Clements-Cortés (CA).

Furthermore, I am in debt to the Editor-in-Chief, Ingelill Eide (N), who invited me to create and regularly write a column on ethics in *Musikkterapi* (the Norwegian Journal of *Music Therapy*). The column 'The Ethics' Corner' has invigorated my mind and sharpened my pen to write on *lived* music and ethics.

A deep-felt thanks to Denise Erdonmez Grocke (AU), who led me *through* music *to* music when I needed it the most. Thanks also to my friends and colleagues Cheryl Dileo (US), Helen Odell-Miller (GB), Inge Nygaard Pedersen (DK), Susanne Metzner (DE), Katrina McFerran (AU), Jörg Fachner (DE/UK), Jaakko Erkkilä (FI), Jos De Backer (BE), Stefano Navone (IT), Torhild Kielland (N), Brynjulf Stige (N), Sigrun Halvorsen (N), and Liv Sandnes Aabø (N) for sharing their lives and academic wisdom.

*Acknowledgements* ix

Big thanks to the excellent Senior Editor Heidi Bishop and Senior Editorial Assistant Talitha Duncan-Todd at Routledge, for your first-rate knowledge, encouragement, patience, and quick responses to e-mails. Moreover, I am in debt to the editors of the *Music and Change Series* for endorsing and working with me on this book, Tia DeNora (US/UK) and Gary Ansdell (UK). Thanks for your scholarly feedback and your inspiring way of giving it.

My deep gratitude goes to national and international students within music pedagogy, music therapy, musicology, and performance-based music studies at BA, MA, and PhD levels, whom I have had the privilege to teach for three decades. You have involved yourselves in debating music and ethics at various levels, which has encouraged me to reflect again—*and again*. Without these repeated discussions and reflections, no book. As a music practitioner, I have met with students, clients, peers, and audiences across multiple music settings. You are why I can write about music and ethics in real-life encounters.

Thanks to Unni Tanum Johns (N) for long-lasting friendship, for sharing academic wisdom, and intersubjective way of relating. And to my mother and father, Marit and Bjarne, who have always believed in me and supported my endeavour. The same gratitude goes to my husband Dag, who encouraged and helped me to take time and space—*and space*—to write this book, and thanks for your excellent cooking. Furthermore, thanks to my closest family Aurora, Ask, Olav, Nora, Marie, Hanna, Hallvard, Åshild, and Halvor. You mean everything to me.

Finally, thanks to the librarians at the Norwegian Academy of Music, who have been most helpful every time I asked for specific literature. Furthermore, thanks to the Norwegian Non-fiction Writers and Translators Association for granting me a scholarship to work on this book. Lastly, thanks to my employer, The Norwegian Academy of Music, for publication support.

Gro Trondalen
Oslo, Norway
26 September 2022

# Introduction

Ethical problems, dilemmas, and unpleasant experiences arise in real-life settings. There may be a friend calling for advice in a difficult situation or when waiting at a bus stop seeing a person losing balance and hitting their head when collapsing. What is sensible advice, and what is the right thing to do in the specific setting? Ethics unfolds as lived experiences in our daily lives and is fundamental to understanding ourselves—and others in the world. It concerns what constitutes a good life. Ethics is about *identifying* a moral dilemma, *reflecting* systematically, to *handle* ethical quandaries based on thorough investigation philosophically, theoretically, and in real-world encounters (Aadland, 2018). Ethics is not a fixed entity; it is fresh produce.

Ethical queries likewise arise in musical settings, theory-building and research in music. A musician may have acquired some information about the performed music's composer, which she/he cannot reveal. A music therapist may have to choose between patients in palliative care due to limited resources. Similarly, a music educator may know that a parent highly thwarts a pupil's musical training engagement. There are also music examples in torture settings, which raise questions of control and unethical behaviour. As an aesthetic art form, the music is ambiguous and allows for various experiences and interpretations with ethical bearings.

Ethics is an old discipline rooted in Antiquity (Socrates, Plato, and Aristotle). However, there seems to be a renewed and increased emphasis on ethics during the last century due to technological development, the professionalization of working life, and globalization (Carson & Kosberg, 2011).

First, technological developments can provide new opportunities and, at the same time, bring with them further questions, values, and choices. Access to music and musical expressions has changed. On the one hand, more people can express themselves musically (perform/compose) through technological innovations and upload their performances on digital platforms.

On the other hand, many people may feel insufficient to access music as the technical devices appear foreign due to its interpretation and reading as software instead of a physical artefact like a DVD or CD.

Second, working life's professionalization may, for example, lead to the performing musician feeling artistically unimportant in a society seemingly less concerned about the value of lived music performances. Some music therapists say they leave the profession because the musical practice seems to lose its relational basis due to efficiency requirements, a time-consuming reporting system, and a financially pressured everyday life. In comparison, music pedagogues disclose they feel alienated in their professional job because music as a part of the human 'Bildung' process (psychological and moral growth of individual character) is increasingly given less attention in curricula in the formative years from childhood to maturity.

The third point about globalization related to music and ethics may foster questions about an instrumentalisation in/of society, which links to issues such as gentrification, gender, racism, culture, and access to different kinds of music. Furthermore, music professionals live in a society where psychological, sociological, political, and personal factors affect their ethical understanding, such as the copyright of music. Therefore, it is necessary to differentiate between the law (legislation) and moral norms and values and where they overlap. Hence, ethics links to multiple discourses and cultural dissimilarities in various parts of the world, where the legislation and culture may diverge somewhat concerning rules and mandates in different countries (Dileo, 2021; Farrant et al., 2014; McFerran & Trondalen, 2020; Stegemann & Weymann, 2019). Consequently, ethics exposes dialogue, offering a variety of endings.

What *is* ethics? 'The core of ethics is, in my view, injustice, signalled by our urge to intervene when we experience something as "wrong," as if someone is offending someone', the social philosopher Arne Johan Vetlesen said in *What is Ethics* (2007, p. 9). The foundation of ethics connects to morality, values, and norms. Ethics is understood in different ways as a discipline, a method, and a practice. As a discipline, ethics defines as systematic thinking about moral problems and connections (Eide & Aadland, 2008) and does not provide absolute and precise answers. Ethics is also a method, a systematic reflection on how things can be right and wrong, good and evil, just and unfair. It is about attitudes, values, and regulations, such as the law. Ethics as a practice then concerns self-reflection and knowledge visible in real-life encounters. It makes the inherent visible and recognizable as a subject of open reflexivity (Lid & Wyller, 2017).

As ethics, music is also defined, interpreted, and understood in various ways. What music is and means in different contexts depends on wording, theoretical and philosophical foundation, and level of reflexivity. From an ontological position, the music itself may appear as a direct experience, acquiring multiple meanings at the moment. The phenomenal music experience emerges as an aesthetic art form—a field of relational lived experiences (Trondalen, 2016). Correspondingly, musical engagement reveals as action and interaction in a cultural and social context, musicking (Small, 1998), meaning any activity involving or related to a music performance. Musicking affords the construction of meaning appropriated by the participants within various contexts (DeNora, 2000). How meaning appropriates depends on the specific setting. For example, musicking in a social context may embrace the uses of music for health purposes (Ansdell & DeNora, 2016; Bonde, 2011; Ruud, 2020) and support new life stories (Bonde et al., 2013). Lived musical experiences offer ways of being, acting, and becoming in the world. Musical engagement and definitions of music make realities with existential influence.

*Ethical musicality* aims at reflecting on music *and* ethics and the crossroads between them. The book is *not* a comprehensive guide to music and ethics per se. On the contrary, it presents some selected perspectives to explore, negotiate, and learn from a music and ethics involvement. This text may be of particular interest to music professionals who want to investigate a philosophical-theoretical-inspired ethical musicality—with practical implications. Yet, it is not limited to this group. It may also offer some ideas of interest to a 'lay' musician and people interested in the topic at different levels of engagement. The book includes no footnotes or endnotes intentionally. However, the references within the text present valuable resources, encouraging further and more in-depth readings.

This book creates from different sources. I am influenced by real-life music-and-ethics experiences as a musician, pedagogue, therapist, musicologist, researcher, and everyday music user. As a teacher and supervisor for master's and PhD students, and a national and international ethics commission board member, I am constantly reminded of music and ethics as *lived experiences in context*. I also appreciate this situatedness in scholarly publications, conference presentations, and dialogues with peers.

I had my upbringing in Norway, a social democracy aspiring towards equal rights for all people, with my academic/musical training within the Western tradition. In my early twenties, I worked abroad and have since then travelled extensively. Accordingly, I am also *privileged* to learn from other people and diverse cultures globally. As a scholar, I have combined an academic carrier with musical practice and research. Music and musical experiences have always impacted me, serving as a life raft and a source of life itself (Trondalen, 2017). My relationship and experiences with music, then, are manifold and have a deep existential dimension.

Seizing, recognizing, and examining my privileges is an ongoing endeavour in my life. I recognize there is no view from nowhere. We all look outwards from within our situatedness, even when aspiring to a meta-perspective. In a conversation on 'Affirmative ethics, posthuman subjectivity, and intimate scholarship', Rosi Braidotti reflects,

> What does it tell you about yourself that you are classified as female, white, middle-class, or LGBT? It is all very useful, yet, not, because what matters to nomadic and posthuman understanding is what kind of ethical subject you are. A subject is a matter of forces, of relations, of capacities, of inclinations. A subject is not a bound entity; it is a relational, transversal threshold of interconnections. How much can you take of the world, how much can you take in? How much beyond the narrow can you go? That is the road to be able to become-world, to become more than just an ego-infested, inward-looking entity. Opening outwards to the world is an affirmative gesture. . . . It is a relational entity – it is you, and me, a collectivity and a group. It is never just one.
>
> (2018, p. 182)

During my continuous reflexivity, I realize that new and opening perspectives on music and ethics *are* emerging and produced. Such an emergence is most visible in the last chapter, where I position myself clearly by entwining music and ethics into a lived *ethical musicality—in becoming*.

That said, the reader might still wonder, what are this book's aims and the rationale behind the selected content?

The book intends to:

1. Offer a selected overview of some influential Western scholars' ideas on music and ethics.
2. Exemplify and explore ethics emerging from real-life experiences within the discipline of music.
3. Propose a framework merging music and ethics into one lived phenomenon, an ethical musicality—*in becoming*.

The book consists of three chapters, interrelated with each other. After offering this brief introduction to music and ethics, the first chapter focuses on ethics as a discipline. Hence, ethics, as systematic thinking about moral problems and contexts, includes ethical theories. Such a music-philosophical discourse, sensible to the human condition of life, elucidates through some influential and selected Western scholars ranging from the *Antiquity* via *modern philosophy* to *contemporary voices*. Some scholars are chosen due to the Western canon (the Ancient Greeks), while others (modern philosophy) are due to their literary influence on the discourse of music and ethics. The selected contemporary intellectuals are influential voices of today. Furthermore, I have sought a balanced gender and age perspective.

Chapter 2 elucidates the musical ethics relationship before contemplating ethics as a practice in different musical real-life settings. Ethical problems, dilemmas, and unpleasant experiences illustrate within the grounds of the performing musician, the music educator, the music therapist, the musicologist, the 'layperson' in her/his everyday musicking and the music researcher. When ethics understands musical practices, it is about reflexivity and acquired knowledge. That is, underpinned by a music-philosophical discourse, which will be demonstrated through the illustrative examples in Chapter 2.

Chapter 3 ties a music-philosophical discourse of music and ethics with musical ethics' practical crossroads towards an ethical musicality—an art of becoming. Such a conceptual framework has existential dimensions, elucidated through cultures of musicality, before investigating the four fundamental existentials (body, relation, time, space), in addition to context, involvement, power, responsibility, sustainability, and hope. When tied together, music and ethics link profoundly, offering real-life perspectives that would otherwise be inaccessible to us. An ethical musicality meets us with a calling *to* humanity in a broad sense. It is an invitation and a welcome to commit to such an aesthetic art form of becoming—offering hope of a good life.

## References

Aadland, E. (2018). *Etikk i profesjonell praksis (Ethics in professional practice)*. Oslo: Det Norske Samlaget.
Ansdell, G., & DeNora, T. (2016). *Musical pathways in recovery: Community music therapy and mental wellbeing*. Farnham: Ashgate.
Bonde, L. O. (2011). Health musicing—music therapy or music and health? A model, eight empirical examples and some personal reflections. *Music and Arts in Action (Special Issue: Health promotion and wellness)*, 120–140.
Bonde, L. O., Ruud, E., Skånland, M. S., & Trondalen, G. (Eds.). (2013). *Musical life stories. Narratives on health musicking* (Vol. 6, NMH-Publications). Oslo: CREMAH, Norges musikkhøgskole.
Braidotti, R. (2018). Affirmative ethics, posthuman subjectivity, and intimate scholarship: A conversation with Rosi Braidotti. In *Decentering the researcher in intimate scholarship: Critical posthuman methodological perspectives in education (Advances in Research on Teaching)* (Vol. 31, pp. 179–188). Bingley: Emerald Publishing Limited. https://doi.org/10.1108/S1479-368720180000031014.
Carson, S. G., & Kosberg, N. (2011). *Etikk. Teori og praksis (Ethics, theory and practice)*. Oslo: Cappelen Damm Akademisk.
DeNora, T. (2000). *Music in everyday life*. Cambridge: Cambridge University Press.

Dileo, C. (2021). *Ethical thinking in music therapy* (2nd ed.). Cherry Hill: Jeffrey Books.

Eide, T., & Aadland, E. (2008). *Etikkhåndboka for kommunenes helse- og omsorgstjenester (The handbook of ethics for the municipalities' health- and care services)*. Oslo: Kommuneforlaget AS.

Farrant, C., Pavlicevic, M., & Tsiris, G. (2014). *A guide to research ethics for arts therapists and arts and health practitioners*. London and Philadelphia: Jessica Kingsley Publishers.

Lid, I. M., & Wyller, T. (2017). *Rom og etikk (Space and ethics)*. Oslo: NOASP, Cappelen Damm Akademisk.

McFerran, K., & Trondalen, G. (2020). *Survey of ethical practices in training, practice, and research around the globe*. Poster presented at the 16th World Congress of Music Therapy: The Polyrhythms of Music Therapy, Online, South Africa, July 7–8.

Ruud, E. (2020). *Towards a sociology of music therapy: Musicking as a cultural immunogen*. Dallas, TX: Barcelona Publishers.

Small, C. (1998). *Musicking. The meanings of performing and listening*. Hanover: University Press of New England.

Stegemann, T., & Weymann, E. (2019). *Ethik in der Musiktherapie. Grundlagen und Praxis (Ethics in music therapy. Foundation and practice)*. Giessen: Psychosozial Verlag.

Trondalen, G. (2016). *Relational music therapy. An intersubjective perspective*. Dallas, TX: Barcelona Publishers.

Trondalen, G. (2017). Profile 44. Gro Trondalen. Norway. In J. F. Mahoney (Ed.), *The lives of music therapists: Profiles in creativity* (Vol. 2, pp. 648–663). Dallas, TX: Barcelona Publishers.

Vetlesen, A. J. (2007). *Hva er etikk? (What is ethics?)*. Oslo: Universitetsforlaget.

# 1 Ethics as a discipline
## A music-philosophical discourse

This chapter addresses ethics as a philosophical discipline and systematic thinking about moral problems and contexts while linking these ideas to a musical discourse. Music and ethics are presented through some influential and selected scholars ranging from *Antiquity* via *modern philosophy* to *contemporary voices*. The issue at stake is what a 'good life' is. In plain text, a 'good life' embeds both the human wisdom of living (skills) and the performance of life itself (good for oneself and others). Hence, a complete and flourishing life has the human condition at the very core, in which music and ethics are essential. The central questions underpinning these elaborations link to the following areas of philosophy:

- Ontology: What are music and ethics?
- Epistemology: How to acquire knowledge of music and ethics?
- Axiology: What criteria of value and value judgements, hence, what hidden and open values and functions comprise the foundation when exploring music *and* ethics?

Embedded in these broad and overarching philosophical questions is the aesthetics of music, embracing questions about its beauty, values, and principles for interpreting and evaluating music as an art form.

The different ideas about music and ethics are offered in an almost chronological historical timeline. However, the historical progress does not aspire to signify a cumulative historical view on ideas of music and ethics per se. The collection of ideas presents a range of facets that are not necessarily historically cumulative. Yet, one move towards the end of this chapter is gradually assembling a history of the humanist tradition in music; it ends by touching upon the present debate of a humanist legacy for thinking about music while encountering posthuman perspectives on music and ethics.

## The Western cradle of music and (meta)ethics

### *Music in the Antiquity*

In most cultures, music plays a unique role in people's life. Interestingly, the meaning, the creation, the performance and even the definition of music vary due to various cultural and social contexts. Music may be seen as a single phenomenon in some cultures, while in others, in union with different art forms such as dance and poetry. In Swahili, for example, the term 'kurchéza' includes a cultural practice including song, dance, drama, and play in a given social context (Bonde, 2009 ). Another example with bearings of relevance to this text originates from ancient Greek, where the term '*mousiké' (techné)* embraced much more than music, as it offered a way of viewing life itself. Initially, mousiké was brought forward by inspiration from the art of the muses. The phenomenon, 'mousiké', was much broader than music; it also integrated the unification of song, dance, word, poetry, and language as an undivided entity. 'Mousiké' then expressed the spiritual culture rather than the physical one (Benestad, 1976; D'Angour, 2021). It was essential in the formation of the human being, for example, development through educational activities. Also, during this time, the human spirit was concerned with existential questions like what *being* and *reality* meant.

For the ancient Greeks, music was linked to ethics in that it was given the power to impose its listeners' ways of living a good or immoral life. Essential questions were handling issues about virtue (*areté*) and human flourishing (*eudaimonia*), in addition to elaborations on the nature of the soul. The relationship between ethics and the arts (here music) was due to art's capability to nurture virtues and human flourishing, be it for the individual or society (Phillips-Hutton & Nielsen, 2021).

### *Pythagoras, the pythagoreans, and the music's ethical power*

The philosopher, Pythagoras of Samos, enters this ancient Greek scene in *c.* 570 BCE. He is associated with discovering that musical intervals can be analyzed in numeric ratios. The early Pythagoreans then attributed music (as they did with numbers) a comic and ethical significance, namely a metaphysical theory. 'Music was esteemed as a tangible earthly counterpart of the mathematical patterns of the universe and the ratios of musical attunement were believed by Pythagoras and his successors to reflect the principle of cosmic order, the so-called harmony of the spheres.' (D'Angour, 2021. p. 117).

'Harmonia' was the cosmic power creating unity, which symbolized the divine and the origin of everything. Even the planets, through quantities in the movement, played together in the 'music of the spheres' (*musica universalis*). This harmony of the spheres was not audible in a usual sense, only heard by the soul. Also, the music was subject to the laws of the numbers characterized by a pre-set order of proportions and beauty. Accordingly, music supported the human being to recognize the cosmos; the meaning of everything was available through music (Sundberg, 1980). In Antiquity, the aesthetics, which connects to the perception of beauty and taste and the nature of art, was included in one unity embedding the beauty itself, the truth and the good, as one undivided entity. The term stems from Greek *aestheticos* and relates to the ability to sense through hearing, sensing, feeling, and noticing (De Caprona, 2013, p. 594).

The Pythagoreans believed strongly in the power of music and the connection between spiritual life and music. They believed music to be the highway to catharsis (purification) or cognitive recognition, as music offered insight into the basic principles of life. The music experience became a path of cognition and a therapeutic means (Varkøy, 1993). It is worth noticing that the Pythagoreans were known for including female scholars, as opposed to other schools of philosophy in ancient Greek. Unfortunately, there seem to be hardly any written submissions of their work (Heyerdal, 1994).

In Antiquity, different music scales and variety in instruments were supposed to ease and bring peace to our minds (e.g. the Doric scale, the instrument lyre) or incite passion (e.g. the Phrygian scale, the instrument aulos, i.e., an ancient Greek wind instrument) (Benestad, 1976). Music scales and instruments acquired the power to regulate the mood, feeling, and emotion evoked in the listener. The *music* then both expressed and affected a person's character. Moreover, the definition of morality and beliefs in life, the 'doctrine of ethos', had a formative *ethical* power (Bengtsson, 1977).

Accordingly, music always meant something to the soul, as music constantly influenced the listener positively or negatively. Such a linear progressive understanding with a pre-set order gave the music ethical power to restore the spiritual balance in a human being, creating a functional person. The music supported harmonic personalities, characterized by the good and beautiful. On this basis, music as an ethical tool obtained space in the pedagogical upbringing of a person (Varkøy, 1993).

## *Plato and Socrates: carriers of tradition*

The philosopher Plato (427–357 BCE) came from an aristocratic heritage, which offered him the privilege of the free citizenship of Athens, and hence the opportunity to meet with Socrates, the very first Greek philosopher who was a native Athenian. In line with his teacher and fellow traveller Socrates (469–399 BCE), whom he joined in his 20s, Plato upgraded music as a means of mind and character building. The musical doctrine of ethos influenced him: music contributed to the upbringing of harmonious people cultivating the good and the beautiful in life, an ethical life. Music was given the power to shape moral attitudes and social life broadly.

Plato holds an essential name within the *virtue theory of ethics*, the oldest of the theories of ethics. This theory does not imply a fixed answer to right or wrong in a specific context. Virtue (*areté*) is about being *good* in a double sense, virtuous as in 'skilled' and virtuous as 'good for other people'. The core value is to act as a wise person would do. The four cardinal virtues are prudence (wisdom), fortitude (courage), temperance (moderation), and a sense of justice (fairness) (Heyerdal, 1994). Also, practical knowledge and wisdom (*phronesis*) following the Cardinal virtues may guide us towards which action to be the right at a specific time. A virtuous action then is situated, as developing a person's character is a lifelong project (Vetlesen, 2007).

From Plato's texts, we know that Socrates meant music was much more essential than any other discipline within the arts (Benestad, 1976, p. 18). The music's character had a unique ability to build personality so that life became meaningful and targeted. Socrates' philosophical ambition was ethical and fulfilled in dialogue with his fellow people. His art of being was to ask and dialogue; in this way, he aimed to awaken and educate people to reflexivity and thereby increase their field of knowledge (*epistêmê*). Such a Socratic method was both an awakening and an educational activity.

Music suffused Plato's work. In *The Laws* (book 2), and not least in his work *The Republic* (books 3 and 10), he dedicated music to a significant role in the upbringing of young citizens, as he believed that music influenced the soul, through either 'good' music or 'bad' music. This view is evident in one of Plato's dialogues between Plato's brother Glaucon and Socrates (Plato, 1969, Rep. 3.401d):

> [E]ducation in music is most sovereign, because more than anything else rhythm and harmony find their way to the inmost soul and take strongest hold upon it, bringing with them and imparting grace, if one is rightly trained.

Education refers here to a collective view on upbringing in society instead of an individual family setting.

Music was a crucial step on the life-long road to the essential podia, philosophy, due to philosophy's status as the highest form of knowledge (Benestad, 1976). As knowledge was the core of ethical and morally correct life, feelings were scaled down in such an upbringing. Knowledge is thus a qualification for a morally right life and something we can acquire. In other words, virtue (*areté*) can be learned (Skard, 1994).

It is noteworthy that there were strict rules for artistic expression even within the music due to the underlying belief that total freedom for the arts led the people astray, away from the 'good life' (Heyerdal, 1994). From an ethic's point of view, interpretations of good or immoral were dominated by the prevalent forces of the time, interpreted by the political, philosophical, and cultural elite of Ancient Greek.

### *Aristotle: an educator*

Aristotle (384–322 BCE) was a most dedicated spokesman of the *virtue theory of ethics*, which implies modelling a virtuous person through its fundamental knowledge of wisdom, moderation, courage, and a sense of fairness (Amundsen, 1994). In addition to Plato, he is the philosopher in Antiquity with the most vital link to music education. Aristotle argued that we are always influenced by music, either positively or negatively. He rejected the 'music of the spheres' (the transcendent world), seeing music as a phenomenon of experience. Hence, the music's influence was empirical and intrinsically linked to a moral character (Benestad, 1976). Unlike Plato, Aristotle claimed music was for recreation and pleasure, not exclusively for educational purposes (D'Angour, 2021). Also, he argued that it is possible to acquire the proper knowledge or insight without taking the right action.

Another aspect worth noticing is Aristotle's link between the metaphor 'catharsis' and music, that is, the music's ability to 'purify' the soul. Catharsis stems from the Greek *kátharsis*, which means 'purification', which is derived from *kathάros*, that is 'clean' (De Caprona, 2013, p. 940). By intensifying and surrendering to different emotions, underpinned and strengthened by a specific set of scales and melodies representing the *same* emotions, assumingly, the exaggerated experience led to cleansing or clarification. This use of music is the opposite of the regulating tradition and practice performed by the Pythagoreans, such as offering calming music to an overstressed mind (i.e. music representing *the opposite)* (Benestad, 1976; D'Angour, 2021).

## Modern philosophy

### *Kant: the categorical imperative and aesthetics*

The Age of Enlightenment emerged during the 17th and 18th centuries, focusing on scientific methods and political and philosophical discourse. This intellectual and philosophical movement showed an increased belief in reason, the Age of Reason. Within this intellectual movement came the

German philosopher Immanuel Kant (1724–1804), inspired by Plato and Aristotle. He explored ethics through moral action, looking especially at the tension between reason and human inclination and preference; he committed to an *ethics of duty*.

The ethics, then, is rule-based, supporting universal and absolutistic norms. Such duty-based ethics was exemplified by Kant formulating a principle for moral handling, *the Categorical Imperative,* which he conveyed in two ways. The first statement is a purely formal or logical one, saying: 'Act only according to that maxim by which you can at the same time will that it should become a universal law'. The other principle focuses on morality: 'So act as to treat humanity, whether in your own person or in another, always as an end and never as only a means" (Britannica, 2020, para 1).

We must act following principles recognized by duty, Kant argues, rather than feelings or an anticipated fruitful outcome. The rule-based, universalistic and absolutistic action comprehends the motive or means as a determinator of its moral value (Storheim, 1993). The source of such an insight is humanity's rational capacity; that is, the imperative is governed by a principle recognized by reason rather than an anticipated outcome or the feeling of doing the right action. In plain text, the assertion of specific, inviolable moral laws means that one must *recognize* what is right, *desire* to do right, and *do* right (Hill Jr, 2013).

Kant was also concerned with the arts and musical judgement, especially the intellectual formalist aspect of listening. However, he was dubious about the aesthetic worth of art, especially music. There seem to be various reasons for Kant's low music assessment (Higgins, 2011). In the 18th century, there was a shift in attention from expressing music to hearing music. Accordingly, elaborations about the music's beauty and human enjoyment (*plaisir*) became apparent (Benestad, 1976).

The German philosopher was inspired by the father of the modern understanding of *aesthetics* as a distinct field of philosophical inquiry, Alexander Gottlieb Baumgarten (1714–1762). As opposed to the matrix of thoughts more traditionally (i.e. art imitates nature), Baumgarten's project was to investigate the judgement of taste ('science of the sensible knowledge'), the beauty of taste beyond the limitations of art. Baumgarten suggested investigating the object through *sensible* knowledge based on feelings of pleasure, which was unrestrained from rational intellectualism. It was only later that the term aesthetics was restricted to the discussion of beauty and the nature of the fine arts.

Kant applied Baumgarten's term aesthetics to the whole area of sensory experiences; beauty is one skill to reason without performing the actual reasoning itself. Accordingly, the beauty itself does not affect our reasoning, as the reflection comes afterwards (Benestad, 1976). When looking more closely at the arts as sources of knowledge, Kant argues that 'music occupies the lowest place among the beautiful arts . . . because it merely plays with sensations'. At its best, music would be 'agreeable' (in Matherne, 2014, p. 135). Interestingly, one of today's philosophical examiners of Kant's expressive theory of music, Samantha Matherne (2014, p. 130), defends what she takes to be Kant's coherent account of music, arguing that 'music can be experienced as *either* agreeable *or* beautiful depending on the attitude we take towards it'.

## Løgstrup: the ethical demand

The Danish theologian-philosopher Knud Ejler Christian Løgstrup (1905–1981) represents *relational ethics*. Løgstrup elaborates on his modern moral philosophy in the book *The ethical demand*. The phenomenologically influenced author sets the tone in the very first sentence of the text (Løgstrup, 1956/1997, p. 8): 'It is characteristic of human life that we normally encounter one another with natural trust'. He makes *trust* an ethical phenomenon belonging to human existence, presupposing that communication always involves trust as the fundamental basis.

The practice of trust is never without risks because 'To trust, however, is to lay oneself open"', Løgstrup claims (p. 9), that is, laying open her/his vulnerability. On this basis, Løgstrup declares his ethical demand, 'A person never has something to do with another person without also having some degree of control over him or her' (pp. 15–16). The demand is silent, radical, one-sided, and not subject to accomplishment. This ethical demand, with its inherent content, is not derived from any universal norm (utilitarian) or rule (Kantianism). On the contrary, Løgstrup argues it is *human* to meet each other with natural trust; there is only *human* morality. The ethical demand then is to comprehend the given and ubiquitous trust, as we cannot exist without this trust. We are mutually dependent on each other, as we are already involved by being confronted with another human being (Vetlesen, 2007).

Løgstrup elaborates and extends his argument by recognizing spontaneous and intuitive phenomena like trust, mercy, and sincerity that are fundamentally other-regarding as a unique relationship ('the sovereign expressions of life', Løgstrup, 2007). These sovereign expressions of life are based neither on reason or actions influenced by a possible outcome nor on results of a specific will. Morality, then, is not rooted in principles and ethical codes, as the right actions are unique in every context, including physical and geographical surroundings and the personal web of values and thoughts. Conversely, when spontaneous expressions of life do not seem valid enough, *reason* must investigate them. Values are as unique as fingerprints (Aadland, 2018). Accordingly, one must act per the values in play, the relational interplay, and the specific context.

## Lévinas: the face of the other

Another representative for *relational ethics* is the French philosopher of Lithuanian Jewish heritage, Emmanuel Lévinas (1905–1995). Lévinas' ontological position is ethics as *first* philosophy (Lévinas, 1989). Such a viewpoint contrasts traditionally first philosophy denoted either metaphysics or theology, including human intention, needs and lust. Lévinas argues that human sociality expresses in the irreducible face-to-face relation that emerges from seeing the Other as the outstanding and irreplaceable creation s/he is (Lévinas, 1961/2012, 1991/1998).

Lévinas claims, unlike Kant, that ethics does not spring from specific actions of moral codes; it begins with *seeing* the Face. It reflects in the term '*eidein*' (from Greek), which means both seeing and understanding, which are two sides of the same coin (Herbst, 2013, p. 48). However, it is about more than seeing and understanding. The complete understanding of the philosophical Face includes an aesthetic dimension: once you have understood, you can see. In this sense, the highest insight, philosophically speaking, is not possible without this double meaning of seeing.

Lévinas claims that we approach each other with a calling, which requests a response. We are called to responsibility through the revelation of the Face. It is an obligation to be there for the Other. Subjectivity is formed in and through our subjection to the other (Lévinas, 1991). Within such a face-to-face encounter, the Other makes me to something that I am not able to become or experience on my own: I am made receptible *and* responsible (Henriksen, 2007). That is, we owe the Other everything, and the Other owes us nothing. Lévinas claims, 'The Other precisely reveals himself in his alterity, not in a shock negating the I, but as the primordial phenomenon of gentleness' (Lévinas, 1961/2012, p. 150). Hence, the Other does not disclose h/himself in a way that reduces to sameness, as the Other is not understandable and cannot be made into an object of the self.

From a philosophical point of view, we can never expect the other to relate in a similar way as we do ourselves. Lévinas (1991, p. 84) specified,

> I have always taken one more step towards him—which is possible only if this step is responsibility. In the responsibility which we have for one another, I have always one response more to give.

The approach to infinite responsibility is radical and presupposes that all interactions between human beings involve presence, trust, and care.

## Langer: philosophy in a new key

The American philosopher Susanne Katherina Knauth Langer (1895–1985) is known for her theoretical work addressing the human mind's meaning-making process through the arts as a fundamental form of human endeavour—by investigating music as a symbolic form (Levitz, 2021). Langer argued that aestheticians in the Western classical tradition for too long had addressed the problems of the arts (and music) primarily based on claims of a metaphysical character, that is, on the premises of empirical science. From a discursive point of view, what should serve as legitimate sources for meaning-making, appropriate values, and ethical reflection?

In her book, *Philosophy in a New Key* (1942/1974), Langer offers a philosophically founded theory on symbols and symbolic transformation as a way for the human being to express themselves in the arts. With inspiration from the neo-Kantian philosopher Ernst Cassirer, Langer highlights two ways in which symbolism presents. We find 'discursive' symbols in the logic, scientific, and everyday language. While human and artistic expressions occur through 'presentational' symbols found in art (music), rituals, and mythmaking, which cannot articulate in a common verbal language. According to Cady (2005, p. 26), Langer's point is that 'humans have experiences, ideas and conceptions ahead of the development of language adequate to express them'. Therefore, these forms of human activity should be regarded as immediate expressions of human values and considered as significantly crucial as language. Furthermore, the experience itself explores human fulfilment, which is relevant to ethical reflection.

Langer's work concerned making sense of the music experience through its structure ('the significant form') (1953/1973). She saw music as an audible tonal analogy to the human world of feelings. In her works, Langer (1942/1974) proposed a way of thinking about the arts focusing on seeing one entity in terms of another. For example, one chord in a specific piece of music does not have a fixed meaning outside its composition. On the contrary, the chord may be used to express a completely different meaning in another tune. Meaning-making comprehends within the context of the specific music. Hence, the symbolic transformation becomes a vital activity for the listener, as it paves the way for human knowing and understanding.

Another characteristic feature with ethical bearing is the value-based recognition of the lived experience, which paves the way for meaning-making rooted in implicit knowing. First, such a validation endorses the human lived experience of *time*. Langer (1953/1973) identified that music is listened to, or performed, within a *timeframe*. She offers two kinds of temporality in music: 'felt time' and 'clock time', of which musical time exclusively connects to the *subjective experience* of 'felt time'. We find ourselves within a musical field where the 'clock time' no longer reigns supreme. Grasping time as a particular aspect of the subjective experience opens for recognizing the human being per se, no matter mental, physical, or social position in life.

16  *Ethics as a discipline*

Second, by validating art (music), rituals, and mythmaking Langer recognises the immediate influence of a music experience on human significance and understanding, hence, of value to ethical life. For example, listening to music supports images like inner pictures, bodily experiences, feelings, thoughts, and memories that might emerge (Bonde, 2007). In a processual meaning-making process, the 'presentational' symbols (Langer, 1942/1974) offer meaning implicitly. The music experience communicates meaning in multiple ways during music listening without the necessity of consciously reflecting upon the lived experience. As the social psychologist Durig states, 'The trust of Langer's work is that logic and meaning exist on a nondiscursive level of emotions' (1994, p. 254). Such meaning-making is a vital symbolic transformation activity for the music listener, as it embraces the totality of being human. These inherent musical experiences may embed a set of open and hidden values, morality, authenticity/ autonomy, and, also, justice, and consequently, open to ethical discussion with different consequences. Music and ethics are not fixed entities from ancient times; they are vigorous experiences 'in a new key', to paraphrase Langer.

## Contemporary voices

### *Nussbaum, human vulnerability, and mercy*

The American neo-Aristotelian philosopher Martha Craven Nussbaum (b. 1947–) accentuates human values such as vulnerability and mercy, and the intelligence of emotions (Nussbaum, 2003). From a political point of view, she belongs to the field of normative frameworks in ethics and political science, while claiming the humanities are essential when forming a healthy democratic society. She associates with the 'Capability Approach', historically referred to as 'Human Development Approach' (Nussbaum, 2011). Nussbaum builds upon and expands the economist and philosopher Amartya Sen's 'Capability Approach' (Sen, 1985/1999) as she accentuates the individual human dignity (Nussbaum, 2011), grounding her theory in Marx and Aristotle. Nussbaum emphasizes the humanistic endeavour as means to a flourishing and virtuous life.

In her Capability Approach, she suggests a list of ten central human functional capabilities to prevail in human dignity. These capabilities rest on the ethically informed pillars of *freedom* and the power to understand humans in their competencies and functions. Nussbaum's list of capabilities may be seen as freedoms protected by law and viewed as needs. And indeed, they relate to values. In Nussbaum's list of the central capabilities, play is listed as number nine of the ten capabilities in her theory on analysing the human condition: '*Play*. Being able to laugh, to play, to enjoy recreational activities' (p. 34). Play, in this sense, is truly embedded in a musical activity, expressive or receptive.

'To be a good human being', Nussbaum said in an interview at *The New Yorkers* (2016, para 11), 'is to have a kind of openness to the world, the ability to trust uncertain things beyond your own control that can lead you to be shattered'. She said that music offered insight into her personality and emotional life, revitalizing a Stoic theory based on no split between thoughts and feelings. The music then becomes decisive for our capability to acknowledge our human vulnerability.

In a recent publication, Nussbaum (2021) introduced 'mercy' in music. She differentiates between two kinds of mercy, of which both link to her analyses of the music work. One type of mercy is presented with a top-down description; mercy grants from on high, based on an asymmetry relationship (hierarchical) between a judge and a wrongdoer (Christian-monarchical tradition). Then mercy arrives as a gift. The other type is egalitarian conceptualization (Graeco-Roman). Here, mercy is settled based on our human condition, as we all have human weaknesses and circumstantial limitations. Recognizing our vulnerable existence links mercy to compassion through the heart's imagination. Furthermore, Nussbaum highlights the difference between compassion and mercy and adds 'sympathetic imagination' as a vital link between them to move 'beyond the doomed strategies of anger and revenge' (p. 819).

Moreover, Nussbaum argues that mercy emerges from the music work (and the text) through the music's structure. As the musical expression is not the same as causation transferred to real life, she addresses the need to look at mercy *i n* (i.e. personalized) and *by* (i.e. textualized, 'the implied author') a work of music. Mercy needs to be explored through the music work; however, also interpreted from a contextual point of view. She poetically argues:

> We need then, mercy. Moreover, when talking seems to lead only to more animosity, perhaps it is music that will take our hearts in hand and lead the way to a world of peace.
>
> (p. 819)

Such a conclusion may be rejected and interpreted as 'only' poetically and metaphorically informed. However, the opposite is the case: her statement is founded on her ethically informed Capability Theory, upgrading freedom, vulnerability, and dignity as pre-conditions for an ethical life (Nussbaum, 2011). Hence, these humanistic values are relevant to the current philosophical discourse on music and ethics.

### Higgins: music as influence and educator

Another philosopher arguing music and ethics relevant to our shared humanity is the American Kathleen Marie Higgins (b. 1954.). She links music to social practice, an ethically loaded activity presented as contextual. Higgins states, while contrasting and elaborating on the structure *within* the music,

> [e]xpectations, models, and responses *are* contextual features, for they can be observed and considered only when one locates musical structure within a context of human expectation that is conditioned by societal belief, thought, and practice. . . . [T]hese are also the bases of music's legitimate claim to have an impact on ethical life.
>
> (Higgins, 2011, p. 8)

Such musical aesthetic features have an intersubjective character within the present experiential context. Higgins highlights that context relates to common beliefs and expectations when encountering the musical 'object'. Furthermore, she accentuates the ethics of music's *social nature*, which contributes to music's important position in our lives. To Higgins, music is first and foremost an *experience*, a vital part of people's lives.

Higgins pinpoints three characteristics when contemplating the music-and-ethics connection (p. 114). First, she argues that music has the psychological power to influence the listener's outlook and behaviour. Such a psychological influence may perform through a sense of ethical agency. Also, a potential musical power might afford and even promote a desirable harmonious interplay amongst people. Second, Higgins suggests music's ability to develop capacities of value to ethical living. Such a facility elaborates on human engagement through affects and intellectual disposition, affording competencies with ethical bearings. Third, Higgins focuses on music's capacity to serve metaphorical and symbolic roles to assist our ethical reflections, that is, supporting revelations of ethical significance.

We need, Higgins argues, guidelines and rules, but not to an exaggerated extent. Guiding principles are necessary but not as generalized rules across different contexts. Besides, music may potentially create solidarity due to its ability to evoke expression and comprehension of what others might communicate (Higgins, 2018). Thus, musical communication might demonstrate the condition of human interactions.

Higgins augments the aesthetic character of living well to music and our ethical considerations from a philosophical point of view. She suggests a positive aspiration allowing for an open-minded, imaginative approach to resolving ethical tensions. Due to its musical nature, such a model may serve as an aesthetic image (Higgins, 2011). Higgins then moves beyond music's universality as she accentuates the music's ability to connect people across different cultures and traditions, hence a sense of a shared human experience (Higgins, 2012). From a philosophical point of view, music becomes both an influence and an educator while essentially supporting a good life and making us more graceful and humane.

### Phillips-Hutton and Nielsen: a consensual model of musical ethics

The Danish Nanette Nielsen (b. 1975) and American Ariana Phillips-Hutton (b. 1987) are other contemporary scholars discussing music and ethics within a musico-philosophical discourse. The chapter *Ethics* (Phillips-Hutton & Nielsen, 2021) explores numerous strands of music and ethics from Ancient Greek to today's elaborations within interdisciplinary contexts of music and ethics. The text draws on current knowledge in *Music and Ethics* by Cobussen and Nielsen (2012/2016) while also pioneering a consensual model of musical ethics. In line with Nussbaum (2003), Higgins (2011, 2012), and Warren (2014), Phillips-Hutton and Nielsen highlight music as a procedural *experience* with various forms of engagement, as opposed to music as a pure 'object'. Accordingly, musical ethics becomes an experiential human way of living, affording insight through processing and engaging broadly with musical and ethical practices and contexts, that is, a musical ethics as a philosophical opportunity, which reveals important aspects of what it means to be both human and humane (Nielsen, 2020).

A consensual model of musical ethics includes the characteristics of being relational, intuitive, embodied, emergent, and practice-oriented (Phillips-Hutton & Nielsen, 2021). The first property of the consensual model is that it is *relational*. Meaning develops in relation to other things, neither as moral relativism nor as autonomism. Interpersonal encounters are essential to promote a good life, as ethics is always embedded in our relationships with others and with ourselves. Ethics elucidates, for example, in a musical give-and-take improvisation, depending on each other's collective responsibility. It is imperative to recognize each person's subjectivity within the multiplicity of musical contexts, as the ethical responsibilities arise from those encounters.

The second characteristic of the model is that it is *intuitive*. The term draws from social psychology's concept of *intuitive ethics* (Haidt & Joseph, 2004), arguing that cultural virtues of approval and disapproval link to patterns of intuitions within different contexts and societies. These innate shared patterns of intuitions develop unconsciously and bind to cultural traditions. From a discursive point of view, music then engages in mental activity beyond any presupposed content and does not reduce to semantics. If music subconsciously influences human behaviour, then exposure to various cultural societies and music traditions may positively shape our empathic responses to others. Subsequently, musical exposure forms our moral imagination and serves as an expression of the intuitive ethical patterns developed by society. Music becomes ethically formative and potentially supportive of a good life, hence an ethically significant practice (Phillips-Hutton & Nielsen, 2021, p. 295).

The third characteristic of the consensual model is that it is *embodied*. When actively listening to or expressing ourselves musically, we become physically and mentally engaged through our movements, breathing, and a sense of vitality. Such an embodied experience influenced by the music's psychosocial power, Higgins (2011) argues, may afford music its ethical capacity (Phillips-Hutton & Nielsen, 2021, p. 295). Embodied experiences through musical engagement offer a sense of being in the world individually and socially. With its inherent vulnerability and sense of being alive, such a being may contribute to ethical reflection and engagement. Phillips-Hutton and Nielsen (2021) draw attention to ways of 'mental offloading' offered by new modes of engagement (Herbert et al., 2019; Krueger, 2019), for example, using devices such as smartphones to regulate physical or mental memories, that is, transferring ('offloading') them to new technologies. Such a mental transformation may occur through both music listening and performance, potentially scaffolding emotional consciousness. As we augment our ethical capacity, music potentially affords new forms of thoughts, experience, and behaviour, offering an insight into a good life (Phillips-Hutton & Nielsen, 2021).

The fourth characteristic of the consensual model is that it is *emergent*. The model highlights time dependency and time sensitivity as the music unfolds in time. However, music becomes more than an 'image of time' (Langer, 1967). As active participants, we continually *become* while negotiating the music's emergent qualities situated individually or socially. Music connects us to a social context, offering a new kind of time consciousness through which our humanity can be affected and transformed. Accordingly, the shared musical experience may provide a social encounter of value for an ethical living (Phillips-Hutton & Nielsen, 2021).

The final characteristic of the consensual model is that it is *practice-oriented*. As a method, it investigates musical practices in line with how people use music in their everyday lives ('musicking'; Small, 1998). Such an approach protects against an overly abstracted reification of music. Additionally, it supports ethical reflexivity within research engagement. Phillips-Hutton and Nielsen claim that 'the primary ethical function of music is to make us more humane by revealing, enacting, and promoting the feelings of ethical responsibilities and sensibilities towards ourselves and one another' (2021, p. 297). Their consensual model links to the thought in Ancient Greek, where the musico-ethical praxis ties contemplation (theoria) to knowledge. Such a process-oriented basis where theory and practice are embodied and enacted in our everyday musical experiences may contribute to and elucidate a philosophical discourse on music and ethics.

## Posthumanism: lines of thought

The final section of this chapter addresses selected *lines of thought*, elucidating the vast and expanding field of posthuman thinking. Such a tangential way of presenting posthumanism, including an illustrative example of practice and research in-becoming, intentionally underpins the paradigm's non-binary and non-hierarchical production *in-becoming*. Accordingly, we intentionally use *they* as the personal pronoun in this section. Hence, this section contrasts the hierarchically chosen presentation of 'tree trunks' of gendered scholars throughout historical time, as previously favoured in this chapter.

According to posthuman philosophy, knowledge produces and interacts *from* the world and *in* the world. Everything produces *in-becoming* due to *collective* processes. Diversity and power relations, non-binary position, and equality are essential lines in such an intersection of human perspectives, ecology, and materiality (the nomadic ethical subject; Braidotti, 2013). They argue that the relational *subject* (the human condition) is produced and positioned together with nonhuman life. Due to its *openness* to other subjects and environments, the human subject is 'mediated technologically or assembled in alignment with nonhuman lives and experience'. Accordingly, Braidotti's position is not in contrast to recent humanist thoughts. On the contrary, it extends such a position (Tomlinson, 2021, p. 417) through its alternative view of subjectivity towards possible transition among identities (Braidotti, 2006).

From this follows an ethical approach produced from the angles of *diversity* and *difference*, a critical posthuman theory leading to a *nomadic ethical subject* aspiring towards recognition of *sameness* (Braidotti, 2006). Further, such affirmative ethics is *embodied and embedded*, containing the seed of its becoming. That is, connecting and intrinsically entangled with material and geopolitical positions (Braidotti, 2018). There is no in-becoming without ethics—and vice versa.

'The discourse of posthumanism is made up of a group of approaches to cultural theory and philosophy that attempt to supersede perceived limitations of the humanisms of the twentieth century', Tomlinson explains in their chapter in the *Oxford Handbook of Western Music and Philosophy* (Tomlinson, 2021, p. 415). The primary sources towards posthuman standpoints stem from studies within science and technology, actor-network theory, animal studies, feminist new materials, and assemblage theory (p. 416). Additionally, re-conceptualization and different tangential thoughts of relationships add to this expanded field of thinking.

What about the ontology and epistemology of music in posthumanism? On what basis is the music itself explained, and which norms and values underpin knowledge production within such lines of thought and territories? Furthermore, does mechanically produced squeaking based on randomly selected algorithms through technological devices qualify as music? Are whale songs and bird calls music? Additionally where and when is material, culture, technology, or semiotic virtuality production-in-becoming? (pp. 421–426). Do music and sound have boundaries? Tomlinson writes (p. 420, with reference to Tinbergen, adapted from Massumi),

> Allowing animal 'song' to help us lose our way with human music would mean experiencing from a nonhuman vantage one aspect of our own supernormality, which would mark a step towards an alienated understanding of what it means to be human.

Similar questions about value-based knowledge and performativity are raised in the different art forms (e.g. Stalpaert et al., 2021).

In current artistic practice, for example in music performance, essential questions are, what does it mean to be human (the music performer) within posthuman lines of thought? When, where, and who is mediating what? What happens when technology, a variety of human and non-human objects and materials, and other living species, intertwine and enact within knowledge-making and a performative practice in-becoming? Where, when, and to whom might a performance, for example, during the COVID-19 pandemic, produce enhanced awareness of our collective condition? One line of thought may support that the performer (the nomadic ethical subject, Braidotti, 2006) aims towards affirmative relatedness, leading towards recognition of sameness. Hence, the music performance embodies and embeds the source of ethics—present in the existential condition.

More strands are endorsed in this section 'Posthumanist performativity: toward an understanding of how matter comes to matter' (Barad, 2008). Barad argues that language is granted too much power as the representation of every 'thing' in practice, theory, and discourse. Moving towards *performative* representation alternatives implies focusing on 'matters of practices/doing/actions'. This line is opposed to the prevailing mirroring of, for example, culture or nature (pp. 121–122). They say,

> In this essay, I propose a specifically posthumanist notion of performativity—one that incorporates important material and discursive, social and scientific, human and nonhuman, and natural and cultural factors.

(p. 126)

## Ethics as a discipline 23

Barad's line of thought implies a shift *from* representationalism *to* performativity. The author suggests a new thread, an 'agential realism', arguing 'rather, the material and the discursive are mutually implicated in the dynamics of intra-activity'. Yet, they are never reducible to one another (p. 140). '"we" are *of* the world. We are part of the world in its differential becoming' (p. 147). Consequently, human and nonhuman, subject and object, mind and body, theory and discourse are all intertwined and enacted as factors that matter in such a fluctuating agency. Performativity, properly construed, is 'real'—in its own right.

How, then, to study the practices of knowing? Barad suggests a 'reworking of the familiar notions of discursive practices, materialization, agency, and causality, among others' (p. 129). They propose an alternative to a discursive division between ethics, ontology, and epistemology. Hence, an *ethico-onto-epistemology*, 'the study of practices of knowing in becoming' (p. 147), as a helpful way of approaching how certain intra-actions indeed matter.

We elucidate with a specifically illustrative example from postmodern thinking in music therapy. This is one example of practice and research in-becoming, one of rhizomatic thinking situated in a post-structuralist line of thought. dos Santos (2020) drew on the work of Deleuze and Guattari (1987/2013), who introduced

> the term 'rhizome' (p. 12) to explain the ever-growing, horizontal networks of connections between heterogeneous nodes of discursive and material forces. There are no fixed positions as a rhizome is made of only lines.
>
> (in dos Santos, 2020, p. 152)

In line with Deleuze and Guattari's (1987/2013) statement that 'music has always sent out lines of flight' (p. 11, in dos Santos, 2020, p. 152), dos Santos suggests musical improvisation to enable creational relational connections and engagement in a group music therapy process. Their research-interest-in-becoming explored the usefulness of aggression in the lives of becoming-teenagers in a local setting in South-Africa (dos Santos, 2020).

dos Santos' rhizomatic research assemblage aimed at producing and responding with the data through a *becoming-response* to the data (p. 161), which is linked to:

- they as a becoming-music therapist/researcher in the relationship, and
- the becoming-teenagers.

Such a non-linear and non-hierarchical methodology in-becoming illuminated connections between concepts in the data material: producing recognition of sameness. Hence, the engendered meaning and significance were produced through socially relevant knowledge *in-becoming* within the collective processes at stake. The intertwining of music and ethics is embodied and embedded *from* and *in* the material and geopolitical positions.

Moving from this illustrative example, while still questioning, what kind of practices of knowing are we talking about, and where, when, and who is involved? What is a good life, individually and socially?

Another line of elaborating on these questions from a critical posthumanistic point of view links to practices of health performance. More precisely, musicking as a *cultural immunogen*, that is, a 'situated practice with possibilities of influencing health and life quality' (Ruud, 2020, p. 47) With reference to a complex and multidimensional sociologic understanding of health/illness conditions (DeNora, 2014), the 'Performance of health, then draws on the resources that are to be found in the environment; it emerges in relation to resources' (Ruud, 2020, p. 47). That is, in relation to our environment and social and economic situatedness. The underlying assumption of music or musicking as a cultural immunogen implies involvement in musical expression or activities stemming from a healthy behaviour in context.

In line with postmodernism, music and ethics are present in such a sociological approach to health musicking as an *interwoven* part of a critical posthuman endeavour located in multiple spaces. An existential 'resonant' relatedness links to power relations and discourse, political, economic, and existential endeavour (Ruud, 2020). Such an assembly of health musicking and ethics comprises uses of music and musicking in our shared and entangled ecological vulnerability.

## Summary

This chapter has addressed a philosophical discourse of music and ethics, linking these phenomena to systematic thinking about moral problems and dialogues in contexts. A philosophical basis has been elucidated through selected thinkers, presented historically from *Antiquity* via modern philosophy to contemporary voices. These ideas' emergence is not necessarily the cumulative progress of ideas throughout time. Instead, they assemble a facet of prevailing ideas influenced by contextual, political, philosophical, and cultural perspectives.

The fundamental questions in this chapter elaborated on the phenomena of music and ethics (ontology) and what knowledge underpinned these beliefs throughout historical time (epistemology). Additionally, the chapter focused on value and value judgement, including different foundations for investigating connections between music and ethics. Embedded in these elaborations are mindsets of the aesthetics of music, elaborating music as an art form.

In essence, in *Antiquity*, music and ethics were intertwined to approach the world. The ancient philosophers Plato and Aristotle advocated the virtue theory of ethics. Music always meant something to the soul as music continuously influenced the listener positively or negatively. In *modern philosophy*, ethics was at the forefront, with Kant advocating ethics of duty while Løgstrup and Lévinas argued relational ethics. Lévinas even claimed ethics as *the first* philosophy, contrasting first philosophy represented either metaphysics or theology. Further, Langer offered a value-based recognition of the musical lived experience through symbols and symbolic transformation, which paved the way for meaning-making on a nondiscursive level of emotions.

*Contemporary voices* augment the discursive field of music and ethics. Nussbaum processes music and ethics, emphasizing vulnerability, mercy, and the power of creating capabilities while Higgins maintains music as an experience, influencing and educating our ethical life. Philips-Hutton and Nielsen enrich the musico-philosophical field by suggesting a consensual model of musical ethics, which includes relational, intuitive, embodied, emergent, and practice-oriented characteristics. Finally, posthuman perspectives present music and ethics through selected lines of thought, illustrating the vast field of posthuman thinking *in-becoming*. Accordingly, contrasting the previous hierarchically preferred 'tree trunks' of thinkers through historical time. Music and ethics are not fixed entities, but ideas and thoughts inspired by the spirit of the time, politics, philosophy, and cultural and social views.

The next chapter offers discursive examples of music and ethics in real-life encounters associated with roles, arenas, and the music profession's self-understanding. The continuous facing of trust, social mission, and legitimacy for the music professionals are illustrated through the performing musician, the music educator, the music therapist, the musicologist, and the music researcher. Also, the 'lay' musician's everyday musicking is included in this chapter.

## References

Aadland, E. (2018). *Etikk i profesjonell praksis (Ethics in professional practice)*. Oslo: Det Norske Samlaget.

Amundsen, L. (1994). Aristoteles (Aristotle). In T. B. Eriksen (Ed.), *Vestens tenkere. Bind I. Fra Homer til Milton (Western thinkers. Volume I. From Homer to Milton)* (pp. 102–118). Oslo: Aschehoug.

## 26  Ethics as a discipline

Barad, K. (2008). Posthumanist performativity: Toward an understanding of how matter comes to matter. In S. H. Stacy Alaimo (Ed.), *Material feminisms* (pp. 120–154). Bloomington: Indiana University Press.

Benestad, F. (1976). *Musikk og tanke. Hovedretninger i musikkestetikkens historie fra antikken til vår egen tid (Music and thought. Main directions in the history of music aesthetics from Antiquity to our time)*. Oslo: Aschehoug.

Bengtsson, I. (1977). *Musikvetenskap. En översikt (Musicology. An overview)* (2nd ed.). Stockholm, Göteborg and Lund: Scandinavian University Books, Esselte Studium.

Bonde, L. O. (2007). Music as metaphor and analogy. A literature essay. *Nordic Journal of Music Therapy 16*(1), 60–81.

Bonde, L. O. (2009). *Musik og menneske. Introduktion til musikpsykologi (Music and the human being. Introduction to music psychology)*. Frederiksberg C: Samfundslitteratur.

Braidotti, R. (2006). *Transposition: On nomadic ethics*. Cambridge and Malden, MA: Polity Press.

Braidotti, R. (2013). *The posthuman*. Cambridge: Polity Press.

Braidotti, R. (2018). Affirmative ethics, posthuman subjectivity, and intimate scholarship: A conversation with Rosi Braidotti. In *Decentering the researcher in intimate scholarship: Critical posthuman methodological perspectives in education (Advances in Research on Teaching)* (Vol. 31, pp. 179–188). Bingley: Emerald Publishing Limited. https://doi.org/10.1108/S1479-368720180000031014.

Britannica. (2020). Categorical imperative. In *Encyclopedia Britannica*. Retrieved from www.britannica.com/topic/categorical-imperative.

Cady, D. L. (2005). *Moral vision. How everyday life shapes ethical thinking*. Lanhna, Boulder, New York, Toronto and Oxford: Rowman & Littlefield Publisher, Inc.

Cobussen, M., & Nielsen, N. (2012/2016). *Music and ethics*. London and New York: Routledge.

D'Angour, A. (2021). Ancient Greece. In T. McAuley, N. Nielsen, J. Levinson, & A. Phillips-Hutton (Eds.), *The Oxford handbook of Western music and philosophy* (pp. 117–135). Oxford: Oxford University Press.

De Caprona, Y. (2013). *Norsk etymologisk ordbok (Norwegian etymological dictionary)* (4th ed.). Oslo: Kagge Forlag AS.

Deleuze, G., & Guattari, F. (1987/2013). *A thousand plateaus*. London: Bloomsbury.

DeNora, T. (2014). *Making sense of reality. Culture and perception in everyday life*. London: SAGE.

dos Santos, A. (2020). The usefulness of aggression as explored by becoming-teenagers in group music therapy. *Nordic Journal of Music Therapy, 29*(2), 150–173. https://doi.org/10.1080/08098131.2019.1649712.

Durig, A. (1994). What did Susanne Langer really mean? *Sociological Theory, 12*(3), 254–265.

Haidt, J., & Joseph, C. (2004). Intuitive ethics. *Daedalus, 133*(4), 55–67.

Henriksen, J.-O. (2007). Emmanuel Lévinas: Den andre gjør meg til den jeg er (Emmanuel Lévinas: The Other makes me to who I am). In K. Steinsholt & L. Løvlie (Eds.), *Pedagogikkens mange ansikter. Pedagogisk idéhistorie fra antikken til det postmoderne (The many faces of pedagogy. Pedagogical history of ideas from Antiquity to the postmodern)* (pp. 528–539). Oslo: Universitetsforlaget.

Herbert, R., Clarke, D., & Clarke, E. (Eds.). (2019). *Music and consciousness 2: Worlds, practices, modalities*. Oxford: Oxford University Press.
Herbst, M. (2013). Blikket, en verden til forskjell. (The Face, a world of difference). *Strek* (4), 46–51.
Heyerdal, G. B. (1994). Platon (Plato). In T. B. Eriksen (Ed.), *Vestens tenkere. Bind I. Fra Homer til Milton (Western thinkers. Volume I. From Homer to Milton)* (pp. 79–101). Oslo: Aschehoug.
Higgins, K. M. (2011). *The music of our lives*. Lanham, Boulder, New York, Toronto and Plymouth, UK: Lexington Books.
Higgins, K. M. (2012). *The music between us: Is music a universal language*. Chicago: University of Chicago Press.
Higgins, K. M. (2018). Connecting music to ethics. *College Music Symposium: Journal of the College Music Society, 58*(3). http://doi.org/10.18177/sym.2018.58.sr.11411.
Hill Jr, T. E. (2013). Kantianism. In H. Lafollette & I. Persson (Eds.), *The Blackwell guide to ethical theory* (2nd ed., pp. 311–331). West Sussex: Wiley Blackwell.
Krueger, J. (2019). Music as affective scaffolding. In E. Clarke, D. Clarke, & R. Herbert (Eds.), *Music and consciousness 2: Worlds; practices, modalities* (pp. 55–70). Oxford: Oxford University Press.
Langer, S. K. (1942/1974). *Philosophy in a new key. A study of symbolism of reason, rite, and art* (3rd ed.). Cambridge, MA: Harvard University Press.
Langer, S. K. (1953/1973). *Feeling and form. A theory of art developed from philosophy in a new key*. London: Routledge and Kegan Paul Limited.
Langer, S. K. (1967). *Mind: An essay on human feeling*. Baltimore; MD: Johns Hopkins University Press.
Lévinas, E. (1961/2012). *Totality and infinity. An essay on exteriority* (A. Lingis, Trans.). Pittsburgh: Duquesne University Press.
Lévinas, E. (1989). Ethics as first philosophy. In S. Hand (Ed.), *The Levinas reader* (pp. 75–87) Oxford: Blackwell.
Lévinas, E. (1991). *Otherwise than being or beyond essence* (A. Lingis, Trans.). Pittsburgh: Duquesne University Press.
Lévinas, E. (1991/1998). *Entre Nous. Thinking-of-the-Other* (M. B. Smith & B. Harshav, Trans. L. D. Kritzman Ed.). New York: Colombia University Press.
Levitz, T. (2021). The twentieth century. In T. T. Mcauley, N. Nielsen, J. Levinson, & A. Phillips-Hutton (Eds.), *The Oxford handbook of Western music and philosophy* (pp. 225–262). Oxford: Oxford University Press.
Løgstrup, K. E. (1956/1997). *The ethical demand* (T. I. Jensen, G. Puckering, & E. Watkins, Trans.). Notre Dame and London: University of Notre Dame Press.
Løgstrup, K. E. (2007). *Beyond the ethical demand*. Notre Dame, IN: University of Notre Dame Press.
Matherne, S. (2014). Kant's expressive theory of music. *The Journal of Aesthetics and Art Criticism, 72*(2), 129–145. http://doi.org/10.1111/jaac.12076.
Nielsen, N. (2020). Den musikalske etik (The musical ethics). In Ø. Varkøy & H. Holm (Eds.), *Musikkfilosofiske tekster. Tanker om musikk- og språk, tolkning, erfaring, tid, klang, stillhet m.m. (Music philosophical texts. Thoughts on music- and language, interpretation, experience, time, sound, silence etc)* (pp. 61–77). Oslo: NOASP, Cappelen Damm Akademisk.

Nussbaum, M. C. (2003). *Upheavals of thought: The intelligence of emotions*. Chicago, IL: University of Chicago Press.
Nussbaum, M. C. (2011). *Creating capabilities. The human development approach*. Cambridge, MA: The Belknap Press of Harvard University Press.
Nussbaum, M. C. (2016). The philosopher of feelings. *Profiles*, July 25. Interviewed by R. Aviv. Retrieved from www.newyorker.com/magazine/2016/07/25/martha-nussbaums-moral-philosophies.
Nussbaum, M. C. (2021). Mercy. In T. T. Mcauley, N. Nielsen, J. Levinson, & A. Phillips-Hutton (Eds.), *The Oxford handbook of Western music and philosophy* (pp. 803–822). Oxford: Oxford University Press.
Phillips-Hutton, A., & Nielsen, N. (2021). Ethics. In T. Mcauley, N. Nielsen, J. Levinson, & A. Phillips-Hutton (Eds.), *The Oxford handbook of Western music and philosophy* (pp. 283–306). Oxford: Oxford University Press.
Plato. (1969). *Plato in twelve volumes* (P. Shorey, Trans.). London, William Heinemann Ltd.; Cambridge, MA: Harvard University Press.
Ruud, E. (2020). *Towards a sociology of music therapy: Musicking as a cultural immunogen*. Dallas, TX: Barcelona Publishers.
Sen, A. (1985/1999). *Commodities and capabilities*. Oxford: Oxford University Press.
Skard, E. (1994). Sokrates. In T. B. Eriksen (Ed.), *Vestens tenkere. Bind I. Fra Homer til Milton (Western thinkers. Volume I. From Homer to Milton)* (Vol. I, pp. 62–78). Oslo: Aschehoug.
Small, C. (1998). *Musicking. The meanings of performing and listening*. Hanover: University Press of New England.
Stalpaert, C., van Baarle, K., & Karreman, L. (Eds.). (2021). *Performance and posthumanism. Staging prototypes of composite bodies*. Cham, CH: Palgrave Macmillan.
Storheim, E. (1993). Immanuel Kant. In T. B. Eriksen (Ed.), *Vestens tenkere. Fra Descartes til Nietzsche (Western thinkers. From Descartes to Nietzsche)* (Vol. II, pp. 242–264). Oslo: Aschehoug.
Sundberg, O. K. (1980). *Pythagoras og de tonende tall (Pythagoras and the sounding numbers)*. Oslo: Forlaget Tanum-Nordli A/S.
Tomlinson, G. (2021). Posthumanism. In T. Mcauley, N. Nielsen, J. Levinson, & A. Phillips-Hutton (Eds.), *Oxford handbook of western music and philosophy* (pp. 415–434). Oxford: Oxford University Press.
Varkøy, Ø. (1993). *Hvorfor musikk? -en musikkpedagogisk idéhistorie (Why music? -a history of the music pedagogical ideas)*. Oslo: Ad Notam Gyldendal AS.
Vetlesen, A. J. (2007). *Hva er etikk? (What is ethics?)*. Oslo: Universitetsforlaget.
Warren, J. R. (2014). *Music and ethical responsibility*. Cambridge: Cambridge University Press.

# 2 Ethics as a practice
## Music in real-life encounters

This chapter has music and ethics in real-life encounters at its very core. The introduction offers a brief account of music, music-ing, and musicking, leading to the current use of music and musicking. Then follows the musical ethics relationship before turning to an exploration of ethics in practice, offering practical examples of music and ethics in real-life music encounters.

Ethical practices in music are associated with roles, arenas, and the music profession's self-understanding. That is, continually negotiating ethical issues linked to trust, social mission, and legitimacy for the music professionals: the performing musician, the music educator, the music therapist, the musicologist, and the music researcher. Also, the 'lay' musician's everyday musicking is integrated in this chapter. Each of the exemplified music and ethics practices presents within the same structure:

- a vignette
- ethical problems
- ethical dilemmas
- unpleasant experiences
- suggested strategies for training of the music student

Interestingly, problems, dilemmas, and unpleasant experiences may be alike in the different music roles and contexts; however, they are not identical. They tie to personal, contextual, and social levels underpinned by diversities in power and experienced truth. The musical practice embraces music as a profound aesthetic resource linked to an ethical commitment. In short, this chapter apprehends making the inherent knowledge visible and recognizable, hence promoting reflection. The virtue music professional strives to act as a 'wise' person would do. That is nurturing human dignity through cultures of wisdom, moderation, and courage while balancing these ethical competencies through a sense of fairness.

Music underpins these encounters. It has different ontologies; what music *is*. One strand of belief understands music primarily as an aesthetic artefact, art in itself (Benestad, 1976; Kjerschow, 1978/91). Music offers an aesthetic value, emerging from the music itself. Linking music to epistemology, David Elliot explores one particular sense of music, 'music as music-<u>making</u> or "music-ing"'. He links what music *is* to what musicians know how to do, the five forms of making music: performing, improvising, composing, arranging, and conducting. Hence, 'music-ing' is the contraction of 'music-making'. Elliot argues, the art of music then, is 'both a form of knowledge and a source of knowledge' (1991, p. 1).

When turning the noun music into a verb, 'musicking' (Small, 1998), the music comprehends as an action. In Small's relational and procedural understanding of musicking, the meaning creates in the interrelated actions that connect to any activity related to music performance in a cultural or social setting. Such situatedness might include controlling the sound machine, performing at a concert, or singing between a mother and her newborn baby. Musicking affords the participants' meaning appropriated within the various social contexts (Ansdell & DeNora, 2016; Bartleet & Higgins, 2018). Accordingly, the relational and procedural experience includes individual, social, and contextual levels.

The current use embraces *music* and *musicking* due to its broader scope than the five forms of making music ('music-ing', Elliot, 1991). The contextual use of music and musicking (Small, 1998) in this book reveals various perspectives at different levels.

## The musical ethics relationship

Music is the hub of a musical ethics relationship. 'Music is, first of all, an experience', Higgins (2011, p. 113) argues. The vital music experience may be expressive or receptive, taking on many forms and interpretations historically and today, with its profound ethical linkages (Cobussen & Nielsen, 2012/2016; Horden, 2000; McAuley et al., 2021). Regarding meaningful engagement of listeners with music and another, Higgins (2011, p. 112) says,

> Western philosophy would do well to regain its earlier insight that music is a profoundly emotional phenomenon. If it did so, it would recognize that the felt sense of engagement basic to musical experience is related to our ethical capacities and orientations.

Music provides an intuitive connection with our emotional life (Nussbaum, 2003), a collective sense of fellowship and solidarity when performing or listening to music. Also, music grasps and extends our emotions mentally and physically to the extent that we may want to dance. Additionally, the music offers an analogue to real life: it is as if the music itself negotiates its way through waves of tension and release (Meyer, 1956), not unlike life itself.

From a philosophical level, Higgins (2011) suggests a linkage between music, aesthetics, and ethics. She accentuates the ethics of music's social nature while maintaining music as an experience, a vital part of people's lives. Higgins links the aesthetic character of a good life to music and our ethical contemplation.

Exploring the musical ethics relationship includes, but do not restrict to, music as an action. A study elucidates by asking, 'Are children able to experience art'?. In his doctoral dissertation, Valberg (2011) examined children entering the symphonic music work at professional orchestra concerts anchored in what he called *a relational aesthetic of music*. He states (Valberg, 2014, para 2, my translation),

> If art is solely an analytical matter for the educated individual with a fully developed artistic 'signature', children have no legitimate place in art. However, if art is first and foremost a relational phenomenon, children have a perceptual state of readiness that makes them suitable and ready for qualified participation from the first moment.

The relational unfolding—and the space for musical interaction—embed as part of the material of the aesthetic object. Hence, understood, analysed, and judged as a formal part of the work of art (Valberg, 2014). From this follows; a musical ethics relationship is a multidimensional aesthetic experience.

From an ethical point of view, such a relational aesthetic of music as an art form affords music experiences as a valid ethical entrance to the art through its appropriations, to everybody, that is, comprising the vital qualities of ethical performance, observable through its focus on the relationship, intuition, embodiment, and emergence (Phillips-Hutton & Nielsen, 2021). Accordingly, music as a *social practice* in context embraces a web of performances from specific fine art settings to everyday use of music. There is a need for contextualization and interpretation in the musical presence when related to ethics, namely, *musical experience as lived*. From a social level, our relationship to music values different kinds of music and ecological relationships, that is, community and culture in a broad sense (Lines, 2018).

## Roles and arenas

Roles and arenas illustrate through examples from music practices. The structure offers a vignette before exploring ethical problems, ethical

32  *Ethics as a practice*

dilemmas, and unpleasant experiences embedded in the illustrations. Additionally, suggested strategies for training of the music student are illustrated.

Musical engagement makes realities, opening for exploring crossroads between music and ethics at a practical level with existential influence. Thus, real-life music in an ethical practice becomes a political, environmental, social, and lifelong professional and personal endeavour.

### The musician: ethics in performance

The following quotes are drawn from two research studies where musicians (19–56 years) from different countries of origin and various primary instruments talked about their lives as music performers (Trondalen, 2013, 2016b). The musicians drew particular attention to the music, their relationship to their chosen instrument, the performance, themselves as persons, in addition to their music training.

## The music

- *Music means everything . . . I am embracing music itself as Life.*
- *Without feelings there is no music and vice versa . . . music gives access to feelings.*
- *Music could 'drain' their [people] minds and bodies—make them open this small room [points to her heart] that most people have closed.*
- *This music [Fauré's Requiem] is lifting us out of the daily life—a taste of Paradise.*

## The instrument

- *The instrument IS my Life . . . I feel the joy of playing.*
- *When I hold my instrument close, I am embracing my love. . . . my instrument is 'my everything'.*
- *I've had a lot of mental and physical problems and challenges connected to playing my personal instrument. Passion is my driving force; the pain is the hourly rate.*
- *It is so difficult to really connect (here: surrender) to the music, as if the scores stand between me and my instrument.*

## The performance

- *I love being a part of an orchestra because it is here [where] the pulse is escalating—it is here it is boiling, and you turn off everything else and it is life and death.*

- *You receive signals from the audience that encourage you to give . . . I am looking for the one smiling face, and I maintain eye contact with that person. From her, I receive a hope for—and expectation of—receiving something from me. It is a mutual process . . . It is a pity that huge orchestral concerts offer so little contact with the audience that is hidden in the dark assembly hall.*
- *[I am] longing to communicate something good . . . [to] offer great music.*
- *Working as a freelance musician I am at the critics' mercy.*

## The musician as a person

- *I'm accepting that I am able to manage. . . . something happened when I recognized that I'm good enough.*
- *Musicians relate to an individual culture, there is a lot of arrogance, however also shyness.*
- *To educate oneself and work as a professional musician is about being in a process . . . I think is it important to develop as a human being if one is to work as a professional musician . . . earlier I was very critical when I heard others play. It has changed. I think I have developed a little—as a person.*
- *It is a growth for life. It takes indeed time to develop as a musician.*

## The music training

- *[I] do really miss open listening to the music as opposed to doing technical analysis in a way that it becomes work, work, work . . . the pleasure is fading away if we're not able to just listen . . . .*
- *I am a bit 'professionally injured' in a way. Earlier I enjoyed the music more. It's a bit sad . . . too much technical listening in the training.*
- *Then you realize that the details you have been cramming in suddenly have meaning in a broader sense: You have grown and expanded as a musician.*
- *My teacher was so enthusiastic; he guided me to the 'music land'.*

Music performance involves several aspects with ethical bearings such as the musician(s), the audience, the music genre, the love of music, the instruments, time, situatedness, rehearsals, scores, and interpretation of the music itself.

*Ethical problems* are recognizable in a musical performance in such a way that may alter the actual music. An uneducated set-up of microphones and technical equipment, for example, often results in a poorly balanced sound reproduction of the instruments, which affects the experience of the music itself. Also, badly visual or audio feedback to the musicians may present a problem and affect the musician's interpretation of the score (Carlsen & Holm, 2017) or the joint musicianship in a band. Further, if the experience of the performed music is constantly second-rated and represented in official critiques, then music as an art form might suffer from the consequences.

Following negative critiques at a more individual level, another problem relates to the musician's mental and physical constraints. An 'aggressive' and 'unpredictable' teacher or conductor may be a problem and affect both the learning and interpretation processes and the musical performance in itself. Additionally, experiencing injuries and, for example, performance anxiety is always challenging. However, it takes on existential dimensions when it affects what means Life to the musician—one's ability to sing or play (Buller, 2002; Decker-Vogt, 2012). Another ethical problem may be the potential cancelling of prebooked and prepaid concert performances. The ethics of duty (the Categorical Imperative informed by Kant), the obligation, may play a role in the musician's decision-making process whether to perform or not. The latter aspects are crucial when working as a freelance musician and there is no substitute. Yet, another ethical problem arises regarding venue owners and organizers who cancel the event on short notice. It affects the musician and the audience economically—such as during the COVID-19 pandemic (OECD, 2020; Røyseng et al., 2022).

*Ethical dilemmas* may arise when using social media platforms to stream performances due to copyright issues and the reproduction of the music. Also, how to deal with an enthusiastic audience member who shares the concert on a content-sharing platform? And as a consequence, based on selected excerpts and a lousy reproduction, newly composed music might be experienced and talked about negatively. The critics might be harmful and affect the popularity and prevalence of the work, hence the composer's professional life.

Furthermore, ethical dilemmas develop encountering an audience, as performance involves mutuality and responsibility (Teixeira & Ferraz, 2018). What is a sensible use of sound and light, less or more? How is it for the musician to be treated as background noise, stop or go on? What kind of repertoire (including lyrics) and stage language to select for different audiences and settings? How to deal with the audience's or musician's misbehaviour? When to stop if something happens on or outside stage? If stagediving, eventually when? Yet, another dilemma: what is respectable and valuable on social media platforms when promoting a musician's freelance business? Is it advisable to use clothes with political and ethical bearing (Trondalen, 2021), when and where?

From a philosophical point of view, one ethical dilemma arises when addressing the relationship between the musician and her audience.

According to Lévinas' relational ethics (1991/1998), the Other (e.g. the audience, other musicians, composer, or similar) makes the musician something she cannot become or experience on her own. She is made receptible and responsible simultaneously. As musical beings, we encounter the Other—in an ethical responsibility. Therefore, an encounter with the Other is an encounter with ourselves (Thomassen, 2019). Warren reminds us, 'Since we are always responsible to more than one person at a time, we will always fail ethically in ethically responding to others'. He wisely continues, 'However, the recognition that musical experience needs to be founded upon ethical response to the other—involving love, trust and justice—will at least mean that the right questions are being considered' (Warren, 2014, p. 188).

Some experiences in the music performance practice neither are problematic nor present a dilemma; they are *unpleasant experiences*. These negative experiences may derive from too little musical preparation or a musician's awareness directed elsewhere than the performance. Others may experience professional reviewers' negative responses or suffer from performance anxiety (Taborsky, 2007). Also, unpleasant experiences may stem from sudden changes in music repertoire, a variety of conductors in an orchestra, different stages and audiences, and the musicians' or teachers' demand for excellent performances (Johansson, 2010; Middelstadt & Fishbein, 1988). Luckily, all these experiences have in common that they all are unpleasant but usually not dangerous per se.

Accordingly, the musicianship *training programmes* include learning strategies for the chosen instrument (Hatfield, 2016; Nielsen et al., 2018; Williamon, 2004) and interpretation (Carlsen & Holm, 2017), including musical, theoretical, and ethically informed reflections of the performance per se (Barad, 2008). It also embeds ethical concerns on copyright issues, performance behaviour, and courses in well-being and self-care, anticipating a carrier as a musician promoting an *enjoyable* musicianship in different contexts. Furthermore, communication skills as a performer embed knowledge of personal strengths and weaknesses, not least if organizing a freelance business. The training then should support a flexible and developing musician identity through individual and group reflexivity (Kim, 2004), aspiring ethical responsibilities in music performance practices.

### *The music educator: ethics in teaching*

*A culturally diverse group of ten students in lower secondary school has music as an elective. They have been tasked to compose a song and choose the genre and lyrics themselves. The agreed plan amongst the students and the teacher was to publish the song composition on social media platforms: the whole composition on YouTube and a humorous video meme* on Twitter. A small group of the students take the lead in crafting a rap with a storyline including caricaturing words about religion (the Prophet Muhammad), ambiguous words (bitch, queer, hell), and drug testing (presented as freedom). They suggest the title 'Fuck you. To hell with COVID'. Three students in the group strongly disagree with parts of the wording. However, they are overruled and then silent.

The example presents *ethical problems* due to the lyrics, the composing process and not least to the agreement of posting the rap on the Internet. A couple of the students are Muslims and feel discriminated against by including caricaturing terms of the Prophet. Similarly, one female student becomes observably uncomfortable when bitch and queer are negatively manifested in the lyrics. The glamorizing of drug testing may be problematic from a legal and ethical point of view.

The illustrative example elucidates an ethical demand; all participants in the music elective should be kept *safe*. Initially, they had all agreed to post the composition on the Internet, but it is an ethical problem that a small group of students are overruled and then silent. One aspect of safeguarding the students is through consent. From a legal point of view, the students are minors. People under the age of majority (usually under 16/18 years) may consent, through an informed assent. Still, the consent must also be obtained by the person's parents or legal guardian (Slotfeldt-Ellingsen, 2020). Hence, the secondary schools they attend have ethical and legal responsibility for the students when they are at school. But do the students involved in the composition process know what informed assent means in a possibly changing posting decision? Legally, they have the right to assent or withdraw at any time, ask for more information about the online posting, and not least have the opportunity to complain to an independent and external person responsible (Dileo, 2021; Farrant et al., 2014). Both safeguarding students (empower, protect, and keep confidentially) and the teacher's responsibilities in all phases of the composition project are multiple and make the foundation for an acceptable solving of the ethics problems.

When somebody in a group suffers discrimination and harassment based on ethnic, social, or religious issues, as in this case, the music elective may present a toxic workplace culture, which is an ethical problem. The respect for personal autonomy, generosity, and even justice may be affected. Also, if the rap were posted on YouTube, exposed at a general level, and interpreted as blasphemy, the group might experience potentially dangerous reactions. Still, people officially exposing themselves as spiritual, no matter their religion, might provoke anger and threats in many countries and contexts.

*Ethical dilemmas* materialize in the example as values conflict in the social classroom practice and in society (Bordieu, 1998), and all reasonable solutions have disadvantages. One dilemma is, should the rap with its content be approved or rejected in its present form? On the one side, the students have created the rap themselves. And most students in the group consider the composition, with its storyline adequate, and in line with the rap genre. Due to religious, social, and individual opinions, the minority does not approve. Both open and hidden values are at stake (Nielsen & Dyndahl, 2021). Should the teacher intervene and suggest some privilege? If so, in what way does such intervention respect and empower the students' musical agency (Karlsen, 2011), their embodied experience of music-making (Merleau-Ponty, 1945/89; Small, 1998), their relational agency of intersubjectivity (Bruya, 2008), and their socio-cultural engagement to the given task (DeNora, 2000)?

We live a digitalized everyday life; we are simultaneously visible and invisible (Skårderud, 2003). The students would be exposed to YouTube and Twitter. How does this un/visibility posting affect the students and the teacher in an ever-increasingly digitalization and sometimes alienation of human dignity in the media? Hence, the musicological discourse may also face ethical dilemmas, where both musical views and intersubjective relationships, not least from a music listener perspective, apply (Cobussen & Nielsen, 2012/2016).

Technological developments provide new opportunities and, at the same time, bring with them further questions, values, and choices. Which benefits and risks of technology usage are at stake? For example, young students can express themselves musically (compose) through technological innovations and easily upload their compositions on digital platforms. However, technological postings may also lead to exclusion and provoke anger and threats in many contexts. Interestingly, music technology per se can also contribute to philosophical considerations, if available (Kosteletos & Georgaki, 2014).

The experience within the group process of composing also includes *unpleasant experiences*, especially for those raising their voice in protest. Raising one's voice supports personal agency. However, it comes with a prize: making oneself open to vulnerability. During the composition process, the teacher took a withdrawn role. Afterwards, the rap experience was used as an event of reflection. When investigating one's ethical views and boundaries, there is a need for a vital and ethical reflexive teacher to allow for and contain cultural and personal diversities to be revealed, clarified, and negotiated in the group. Therefore, the teachers should know and negotiate their situatedness (Westerlund et al., 2021).

Using the rap experience for exploration demands reflection from each student due to the musicking's ambiguity. The students may be emotionally affected and feel discomfort when evaluating the composition process, since the rap genre does not present a clear stand of morally right or wrong. Making the invisible visible might support a frame of reflexive ethics, increase awareness and new understanding in the student group, as ethical thinking comes with practice. An ethical endeavour is thus an exercise of otherness; see the other in her/his uniqueness (Jourdan, 2012; Krüger, 2020; Lévinas, 1991/1998). Maybe the event at stake might be enriched by exploring *one* way of initiating the philosophy of religion 'multiculturally', namely, introducing an adoption of the code from the Hawai'i's elected king Kalākaua: 'Thread carefully, don't overstep the boundaries, don't be too hasty to assume you understand, let empathy be your closest companion' (in Griffith-Dickson, 2012, p. 88).

Accordingly, respectful and inclusive ethical conflict resolution is a necessary part of the professional *training programmes in music education* (Allsup & Westerlund, 2012). Reflective ethical practice *within* the educational situations; hence, an experience in handling disagreement may be seen as a teaching model in itself. Accordingly, music as an intercultural tool in the culturally diverse classrooms may support intercultural education *through* an inclusive music pedagogy (Rinde & Christophersen, 2021).

During professional music education training, the institution evaluates the students' suitability for future employment. Suitability comprehends much more than acting according to the Law or a Code of Ethics. It is associated with the profession's self-understanding, the reflexive music practitioner. Therefore, suitability also involves social mission and legitimacy (Kildahl, 2020). Ethics in training programmes in music education then concerns both self-reflection and knowledge. It apprehends making the inherent knowing visible and recognizable as a subject of open reflexivity to future music educators.

### *The music therapist: ethics in therapy*

*Tri is 19 years old. She is referred to music therapy in an outpatient setting due to mental health difficulties, including depression and sporadically substance abuse. The music therapy has lasted for two months (eight sessions), and both expressive and receptive methods have been used interchangeably. Eventually, the client and therapist decided to collaborate on a playlist to support Tri in her everyday life. The client brought her familiar music from the heavy metal genre to the current session. Tri implied that some persons at a closed membership forum on a social media account had suggested some of the music. While listening to the actual music in the session, the music triggered Tri's negative thoughts and aggressive way of thinking, in addition to her substance craving. Eventually, it became evident that Tri had used the same music during self-mutilation and substance abuse.*

The example presents *ethical problems* due to the client's experience of listening to her chosen music: trigging her substance craving and her

*Ethics as a practice* 39

negative state of depression. What happens when potentially positive and motivational music experiences link to 'old difficulties' of drug abuse, with which depression was also associated? Even in a safe and motivational setting, the music experience may influence a setback in the actual health-promoting practice that music therapy represents to Tri.

Research in neuroscience shows that music is treated by brain structures closely linked to emotions, motivation, and reward systems. For example, strong music experiences trigger dopamine, a neurotransmitter that plays a crucial role in reward-based learning (Moore, 2013; Salimpoor et al., 2011). Therefore, it is vital to investigate the client's music preferences linked to the music associated with *positive* experiences. Recent brain research also shows that enjoyable music experiences are handled in the same brain reward capacities as euphoriant drugs. Consequently, 'one has to be cautious and conscious of the emotional impact that music can provide' (Fachner, 2017, p. 14).

*Ethical dilemmas* occur in the example. Would it be appropriate to listen to the client's music when it is not given in advance whether the client will experience a decrease or an increase in substance behaviour and depression when listening to her preferred music (Short & Dingle, 2015; Aalbers et al., 2017) or not? The client might even have experienced a positive link between the music and the use of drugs at one point. Is psychological distress more at risk when listening to metal music than other music genres (Hines & McFerran, 2014)? When struggling with depression and handling low, some people might want to dwell on feeling unhappy. In such a state of mind, listening to music may lead to an even more depressed state, but not always (McFerran, 2011a, para. 6).

Another dilemma arises. Music therapy takes a starting point in the user's preferred music when creating the playlist. Such an approach may support 'self-efficacy' and assist the client in developing confidence, motivation, and the experience of having some control over behaviour and the social environment (Bandura, 1986), that is, creating capabilities, which is an ethical endeavour (Nussbaum, 2011). From a musical point of view, musically induced potentials and connotations ('antigens') may include

- vitality (emotional regulation)
- agency
- connectivity (music as a social resource), and
- meaning making.

These 'antigens' are interrelated phenomena and interact, for example, in the essential creation of personal and social identity (Ruud, 2020, p. 3). In what ways is it possible to recognize and support musical 'antigens' for the client in her recovery (Solli & Rolvsjord, 2015) when the client's chosen music seems to activate the opposite of promoting well-being?

Moreover, should the music therapist directly address the client implicating her link to the Internet account, potentially the dark net with its subculture where, for example, music is shared for self-harming or, at worst, suicide (Moland, 2021)? These actions might be understood as ethical dilemmas at an individual and social level and related to a potential musical sharing. Therefore, would it be most beneficial to hold back and wait or explore the dark sources of the musical choices more explicitly? Shame might be involved (Skårderud, 2003), which is a powerful enemy.

The music therapy session includes *unpleasant* experiences—for the client and the therapist. For example, the client may experience that the therapist mis-attunes so that the client perceives her choice, her musical experience of metal music, is 'stolen'. The music therapist exposes the chosen music so the client feels deprived of the experience of being a person who *can* pick her 'right' music. Then, low self-esteem and lack of control might be connected to the music listening experience (Trondalen, 2016a), and both miss out on enjoying a shared experience. Exposure of negative affect and feelings may also influence the relationship in the session. That is, exposing feelings may show a trustful relationship and eventually reduce loneliness (Schäfer et al., 2020). Also, aggression in music therapy may help strengthen creativity (Navone & Carollo, 2016; Pool & Odell-Miller, 2011) and support teenagers-in-becoming develop 'rules for a good living' (dos Santos, 2020).

In the music therapy setting, Tri and the therapist are mutually dependent on the working alliance, inhabiting different roles and competencies. Various feelings are in play. Also, responsibility is differently distributed in a therapeutic setting. The client performs her agency by taking the initiative, exerting control in sessions, committing to the relationship, and engaging across contexts (Rolvsjord, 2015). At the same time, professional self-doubt seems essential for the therapist as a humble and sensitive manner of appearing to assist growth in the therapeutic alliance (Nissen-Lie et al., 2010). Dealing with unpleasant feelings in fruitful ways links to contextual and procedural competencies in becoming.

During the *training of music therapists*, ethics are constantly underpinning the teaching, the music therapy practice (internship), and the students' experiential learning and developmental processes to foster a reflecting music therapy practitioner (Pedersen et al., 2022). The music therapy training also highlights the Code of Ethics, which comes into play and adds meaning when the law does not provide distinct rules. Suitability in the profession is vital.

Positions of power, the music therapy student's adaptability, and infringement of cultural biases should be mirrored in the curriculum and discussed through 'problem-solving' dialogue in the classroom setting and supervision (Dileo, 2021; DiMaio & Engen, 2020; Stegemann & Weymann, 2019). Hence, discursive reflexivity is vital in a constant update of curricula while developing music therapy as a discipline (Brotons et al., 2022). Some relevant questions linking to the illustrative case example may be: what *is* music therapy (Ansdell & Stige, 2018; Fuhr & Stensæth, 2022; Ruud, 2020), what can/cannot music do (DeNora & Ansdell, 2014), can music be unethical, and might self-mutilation to music be interpreted as an aesthetic part of a (postmodern) project of staging oneself?

Ethical awareness links to a contextual dialogue between music, emotions, and well-being, as opposed to a generalized view of the effect of music (McFerran, 2016). In training, the students reflect upon the potential effect of music therapy on increased motivation for treatment, emotional awareness, and social participation outcomes for substance use clients (Carter & Panisch, 2021; Ghetti et al., 2022; Gold et al., 2013). These aspects empower the music therapy student to explore the function and significance of bringing, for example, Tri's musical choice to the therapy session from a user perspective. Hence, an ethical reflection on how to support the client towards new ways of learning to appreciate, reconstruct and incorporate state-specific emotional responses to her preferred music to rebalance emotion and experience reward (Fachner, 2017).

## *The musicologist: ethics in theory-building*

*Four musicians improvise freely together using various instruments and singing. They have professional training in music education, music therapy, composition, and performance practice as a singer. They meet for one improvisation only to provide primary data for a developmental project on music improvisation and theory-building. The musicians are acquaintances of the musicologist carrying out the improvisation project while having only limited knowledge of each other. They all consent to use improvisation as primary data for the musicologist's project. In line with ethical procedure, the participants acquire written information and give their informed consent before the video recording of the improvisation. The study will be reported in the University College's Open Access series on Music, Practice and Theory building. The musicologist is employed as a tenure track faculty member at the University College and must prove a high-quality professional development within a pre-scheduled and limited time. The project report is a required part of the musicologist's obligation to keep her standing within the tenure track. Four months after the recorded improvisation, the singer has second thoughts about participating in the project and wants to withdraw his consent.*

The example presents *ethical problems* even though informed consent was obtained before the improvisation took place, in line with the institution's ethical guidelines. Four months within the musicologist's thorough analyses of the improvisation, the singer has second thoughts and wants to withdraw his consent. As participation in the project is voluntary, he is ethically entitled to do so at any time without giving a reason and with no adverse consequences (Farrant et al., 2014). According to the University College's ethical guidelines for development projects, all information about the singer and his participation in the videotaped improvisation should then be deleted. As the primary data consists of the videotaped group improvisation, the tenure track musicologist would lose her data. She has a problem.

Also, relationships and trust are affected. What happens to friendship when there is an agreement, but one part does not trust or disagree with the other's *professional* endeavour? It turned out that the singer had doubts regarding the musicologist's theory-building aim of the project. He anticipated the musicologist would 'kill' the improvisation with her words (Finley, 2014; Viega, 2016). The singer's view on performativity is challenged; an understanding of 'how matter comes to matter', to use Barad's words (2008, p. 120). Theorizing the artistic work would counteract his view on performativity and eventually influence his credibility as a performer, the singer argues. The problems are evident; the respect for each other's professionality and friendship is at stake.

Several *ethical dilemmas* also occur in the current example at a practical and epistemological level. Should the musicologist persuade her friend to stay in the project or immediately accept the friend's choice due to the participant's right to withdraw without negative consequences? Whatever solution she chooses, the musicologist and the participant are professionally and emotionally affected. Additionally, when the musicologist employs tenure track, time, data collection, the procedure of analyses and finalizing the development project in time comprise constant pressure due to economic, professional, and individual constraints, her faculty position is in jeopardy. Is it ethically acceptable to expose her margins openly to the singer and potentially be perceived as pressuring the participant to stay in the project despite the participant questioning the project's aim or not?

The singer's reason for withdrawing (i.e. his view upon performativity) also illustrates an epistemological dilemma in the music project. Which is ethically and epistemologically 'right' conceptual representation and interpretation of data when art-based approaches (Finley, 2014; Viega, 2016), 'traditional' theory-building (Glaser & Strauss, 1967), and music analyses procedures (Trondalen & Wosch, 2016) are potentially relevant co-creative approaches? The musicologist aspired towards theoretical enhancement and theory-building stemming from the music improvisation. As theory-building usually involves an advanced conceptual representation looking at the data from a wide-ranging and somewhat distant perspective, such an aim of the project involves higher level conceptual schemes than analysis (Thom, 2021). Consequently, musicology produces musical understanding as much as it reflects the different beliefs and opinions (Ruud, 2016). For example, evidence-based approaches are downscaled if value-based evaluation (axiology) is at the forefront of the arts. Accordingly, a musically advanced conceptual representation (theory-building) represents a dilemma with ethical bearing: which values take precedence?

How to stay close to the actual improvisation while apprehending novel representation of the music improvisation? Or maybe the musicologist did not 'distance' herself from the performance, when using a 'grounded theory' approach (Glaser & Strauss, 1967)? In this case, we meet with an interpretivist methodology where the collection of data, categorial coding and analyses simultaneously co-creates in her theory building process. Putting words to an experience is never the same as the immediate experience itself. Furthermore, as ethics links to accuracy and trustworthiness in the project, should the musicologist include the member-check procedure (Lincoln & Guba, 1985), and if so, what and when to check?

The aftermath of the withdrawal comes with *unpleasant experiences*, both for the musicologist and for the participant. The singer experiences negative feelings of being exposed to the current music project. At the same time, the musicologist has a professional task to scaffold her repertoire of interpretation, aesthetics, and theory-building, including clarifying her ontological positions. Such a theoretical scaffolding may influence the ethical 'truths' potentially embedded in the different professional identities represented in the improvisation. Hence, the various understandings of performativity and theorizing the improvisation (artwork) and personal trust are tested. These aspects also elucidate significant ethical challenges when inviting friends or acquaintances to participate in a music project while dependent on their practical cooperation.

A *training in musicology* addresses the relationship between music and ethics and explores a musical ethics (Higgins, 2018; Phillips-Hutton & Nielsen, 2021) with their differences and overlaps. Developing reflexivity in theory-building within the arts is a constant strive, also from an ethical perspective, as it includes epistemology, performativity, creativity, and analytical efforts. Therefore, there is a need for dialogue and reflection on the musical improvisation concerning inherent and biased judgements, for example, embedded in the 'hidden curriculum' (Johansen, 2021) of a musicologist's training. It might also be helpful to re-think how informed an 'informed consent' is?

## 44  Ethics as a practice

Training should also promote a necessary reflexivity process embedded in such a theory-building related to conscious and unconscious use of, for example, a gendered interpretation and language of music (McClary, 2002) and potentially gendered selections of referenced authors. Theory which combines the use of music to the phenomenon of identity (MacDonald et al., 2017), for instance, might affect policymakers and laypeople in their real-life choices, as musical identities link to the vital comprehension of what constitutes a 'good life'.

Investigating an improvisation always includes ethics since the musical event per se is a musical experience of encountering the Other (Lévinas, 1991/1998; Løgstrup, 1956/1997). Consequently, ethical responsibility should be placed at the heart of musical practices (Warren, 2014). Additionally, the expertise of ethically robust developmental endeavours within the arts includes a reflexive positioning of oneself, for example, within interdisciplinary aesthetics (Kruse, 2016). Ethical judgement arises from an artistic, theoretical, and human perspective (Cox & Levine, 2016), including the professional craftsmanship of a musicologist's training.

### *The 'lay' musician: ethics in everyday musicking*

*Arthur is an 83-year-old retired philosopher who values music as essential to his life. He is a regular at concerts and cherishes listening to music in his everyday life. Due to the global COVID-19 pandemic and its influences worldwide, the concert halls and senior centres' performances are either limited or cancelled. He listens to CDs at home, but the music reminds him of his partner, who suddenly passed away the year before. They shared the love of music, so the memories are unforgettable—and sometimes painful. Arthur has limited knowledge of accessing social media platforms and digital devices at a general level. Therefore, he does not have the necessary technological skills to subscribe to live streaming sites (e.g. concerts) or digital music platform services (e.g. Spotify) to add to his music listening collection. Arthur listens to the radio but says the music presented is too limited in genre and musical expression to his taste. Therefore, he most often turns off the radio these days. He feels lonely, and the music on his CDs does not give him the same comfort as before.*

The example illustrates *ethical problems* for the lay musician in various ways. To Arthur, listening is a 'doing', which he often performs at concerts, hence, musicking (Small, 1998). Therefore, the limited prospects or closure of social arenas gives him a feeling of exclusion. Such exclusion is problematic with its implications concerning the ethics of a sustainable and inclusive society (UN, 1948, 2015). Today's society favours people with technological skills, when accessing music concerts such as booking tickets online. In the example, digital affordances became a problem due to a lack of access to and knowledge of digital devices. Uploading new music or listening to live streaming of concerts became no option, which is an ethical problem concerning Arthur's 'good life'.

When losing a loved one, music listening might be associated with health affordances (Ruud, 2013; Schäfer et al., 2020; Vist & Bonde, 2013). However, it becomes an ethical problem when Arthur's access to music is strangled due to digital skills shortage and a lockdown (Carlson et al., 2021). In addition, the music presented on the radio, which might have been selected based on algorithms, provides a problem to Arthur, that is, always more of the same music genre. Arthur then could not appropriate the music neither as a mood repair and a sense of connectedness nor as a refill of his musical reservoir, which used to offer him a sense of well-being in his daily life.

*Ethical dilemmas* occur in the current example. Listening to personally selected and preferred music is associated with positive feelings and self-care (Batt-Rawden et al., 2005; Skånland, 2012). However, the opposite is the case here. Listening to his deceased partner's and his commonly created *musical signature* came with a price, the feelings of loss and loneliness. Would it be ethically satisfactory for Arthur to share their music with some friends, as musical signatures and playlists (here: CDs) are private, a privacy people usually do not share in public? Should he listen to the music and recognize his vulnerability and loss, or should he leave the idea and wait for 'fate' to decide? The underlying ethical dilemmas connect to the complex phenomenon of what music can and cannot do to health and a 'good life' (DeNora & Ansdell, 2014; Phillips-Hutton & Nielsen, 2021). The philosopher Arthur links music to personal insight, human wisdom, and living the 'good life'. To Arthur, such a human flourishing (*eudemonia*) happens in a socio-cultural setting, of which he feels deprived.

The example includes *unpleasant experiences*. Arthur is grieving, which is entirely ordinary and necessary. However, as the music changes from something life-giving and nurturing to exposure to sad feelings, he does not seek out music in his everyday life. A musical process of healing takes its toll—in time. Both unpleasant and pleasant experiences must be included and processed from an existential perspective. Hence, living has loss and grief, no matter age (McFerran, 2011b; Vist & Bonde, 2013). Music may be interpreted as an 'asylum', a 'respite from distress and a place and time in which it is possible to flourish' (DeNora, 2013, p. 1)—in other words, a place and space for resting, playing, and creative activities (Ekholm et al., 2016). Maybe, *in time*, music may offer Arthur a grieving process both as a contained space and through the experiences of music itself. If so, the music presents an ethically informed processual expertise, supporting a complete and flourishing life. Such ethics has the human condition at the very core, in which the discourse of music and ethics is essential.

During the *training of music professionals*, elaborating on everyday musicking, the students should acquire an ethically informed reflective attitude to music and people (Baltazar et al., 2019; Bonde & Theorell, 2018; DeNora & Ansdell, 2014). The literature identifies potential health benefits of everyday music participation, such as creating musical identities (MacDonald et al., 2017) and the affordances and appropriations of musicking as a technology of the self (DeNora, 2000). At the same time, there is a need to act mindfully towards potential harmful use. Examples are using music to increase depressive states (Erkkilä et al., 2011; McFerran et al., 2013) or for destructive ideological purposes (Teitelbaum, 2014).

Technology may be a great tool to advance in musicking and get access to music that otherwise would have been inaccessible. However, due to personal, social, and economic constraints, technological advances are not accessible to everybody. Therefore, training about everyday musicking should focus on an ethically informed approach to music as a phenomenal experience (Gabrielson, 2011; Higgins, 2011; Phillips-Hutton & Nielsen, 2021). Such an approach also involves knowledge of biopsychosocial responses to music (Blichfeldt-Ærø et al., 2020; Vuoskoski et al., 2022) alongside music and meaning at various levels (Ansdell, 2014; DeNora, 2000; MacDonald et al., 2012).

## *The music researcher: ethics in research*

*A group of nine idealistic music professionals trained in different music fields perform a small-scaled multi-cite study on 'The experience of music'. The primary research question is, 'How do a group of people between 20- and 30 years old experience music'? The qualitative (interpretivist) design uses semi-structured interviews as the research method. The procedure of analysis is not yet decided. Furthermore, the research group plans for in-depth interviews with 33 diverse informants recruited and interviewed within six months. The study is set up for two years. In the final part of the study, all the researchers will collaborate on a text published in an internationally high-ranked peer-reviewed music journal. The research group members are equally distributed between a university, a university college, and a higher music education institution situated in Europe (Norway), South Africa, and Australia, respectively. As regards economy, the research group has no external financing for the study, so the researchers perform research within their regular job at their institutions. The researchers individually acquire ethical pre-clearance in line with their countries' legal regulations and ethical guidelines within the project's first months.*

*Ethical problems* arise at different levels. The first problem is the linguistic understanding of the notion of 'experience', which embeds various readings. In Norwegian, for example, the term 'experience' is translated into two words. First, 'opplevelse' means the subjective experience of living through an event. Second, 'erfaring' signifies the knowledge and skills gained by doing something. Another linguistic challenge emerges per the term 'music', which might relate to 'Western fine art music' as opposed to 'musicking' or a cultural practice of song, dance, drama, and play in a specific social setting, '*kuchéza*' (Bonde, 2009). Hence, the concepts and their linkages (ontology) in the different languages represent a problem when aspiring to a precise research question.

At a practical level, data storage and cloud-computing services and the researchers' access to data become an ethical problem due to the General Data Protection Regulations (GDPR) in Europe (EU, incl. EEA, 2018, May 25). GDPR is a set of laws imposing data privacy and security law—everywhere. Ethical problems emerge in the research group since the multi-site effort included Third Parties outside the EU with other data security approval systems than the GDPR directive. The study is delayed.

One *ethical dilemma* emerges when the group discusses data processing. Professional value-based knowledge (epistemology) comes to the surface. Should the data create into categories (layers; hermeneutics) or be merged into themes (essence; phenomenology)? Which value-based considerations should take precedence? Doing research is not a linear process. An example of changing conditions is due to the COVID-19 pandemic. Recruitment of participants presents an ethical dilemma, as the study must move from face-to-face to web interviews. Do these transitions lead to the exclusion of participants who are non-experienced Internet users, or not?

Another ethical dilemma concerns the selection of participants. The research group wants a diverse group of informants. However, to be enrolled in the interview study, the informants need to be able to verbalize their music experiences. A transfer from the implicit procedural knowing to mediated knowledge of the music experience is a considerable leap in mentalization capacity. Thus, which levels of diversity amongst the participants are feasible? Diversity is in jeopardy. Furthermore, it turns out that one country collects interview data very quickly. In contrast, another country is behind. Is it valid research to transfer data from one continent to another to fulfil the number of participants, or not?

*Unpleasant experiences* occur when some researchers must take on more responsibility than others to complete the study. Professional authorships to publications and artwork in the public sphere are due to international ethical standards, for example, the Vancouver Recommendations (1979). As ideas, material, presentations, and publications are the researchers' intellectual property, research integrity aims for 'a high degree of accountability among researchers'. (Hjellbrekke et al., 2018, p. 6). In this study, the order of the authors is not discussed and agreed upon from the start. Due to the researchers' different work efforts, more unpleasant experiences occur when some have reservations about the (non-spoken but anticipated) alphabetic order of authors.

Another issue causing unpleasant experiences is discussions on *where* to publish the study. First, the group has different preferences based on professional identity and their respective field of music professionalism. Second, numerous journals and publishers, including Open Access journals, have high credibility. However, as Open Access publication would involve money, some researchers do not want to pay or cannot pay. Also, some researchers want to publish quite quickly due to a tenure track position or institutional requirement of performing high-quality research within a limited time. In comparison, others do not work under the same conditions. Which considerations shall take precedence?

The foundation of research ethics in *training music professionals* is the principle of *human dignity* (Johannesen et al., 2007). The research student must acquire a foundation within ethical pre-clearance and control, involving Governance and Research Ethics Committees. From a legal and juridical point of view, The Declaration of Helsinki (1964), The Vancouver Recommendations (1979), and the General Data Protection Regulation (GDPR, EU incl. EEA, 2018, May 25) are essential. The student then should be familiar with the Law (legislation and regulations) and ethics (values, morals, virtues) and their overlaps. Importantly, ethics links to several value-based discourses and cultural diversities in different parts of the world, and the legislation may differ somewhat concerning rules and mandates in various countries.

A research practice presents an ethical demand (Løgstrup, 1956/1997); all participants in a study should be kept *safe*. One aspect of safeguarding the participants is *informed consent*, which should be (1) voluntarily (desire), (2) explicitly (say yes) and informed (explained of the risks and benefits), (Dileo, 2021; Robson, 1993/2002). Legally, the participants have the right to consent or withdraw at any time, ask for more information about the research, and not least can complain to an independent and external person responsible (Farrant et al., 2014). Both safeguarding participants (empower, protect, and keep confidentially) and the researchers' responsibilities in all phases of the research are multiple and make the foundation for an acceptable research approach (Stegemann & Weymann, 2019).

Scientific misconduct, fraud, and questionable research practices comprise fabrication (making up), falsification (manipulating), and plagiarism (making up/take others' ideas or results) (Vinter et al., 2016). Dileo clarifies (2021, p. 1231),

> Fraud is distinguished from other types of unintentional actions, such as honest mistakes in typing, calculating, typesetting, referencing, etc., that often are the result of sloppiness or carelessness on the part of the author.

Plagiarism is a challenge in different ways. Many sites today run an online plagiarism check. However, deficient referencing in publications and the fact that a considerable amount of the scientific legacy is unavailable online (not scanned or digitally preserved) cause difficulties in uncovering plagiarism (Torp, 2017). As far as music is concerned, it is occasionally demanding to investigate frauds, as the concepts of what constitutes fraud may sometimes be challenging to decide in the arts. Additionally, nearly the same idea might emerge in different parts of the world as music researchers identify the same lack of scientific or artistic knowledge in the field. Ethical thinking and reflexivity are essential in every aspect of a research process when handling music, material, or people (Banjani et al., 2003; Stige et al., 2009).

The foundation of societal and personal *research integrity* is regulated in various ways and comprises a vital part of the training of a music researcher. The laws, regulations, recommendations, and guidelines direct music researchers. Fundamental principles of research integrity presented, for example, in the European Code of Conduct for Research Integrity are reliability, honesty, respect, and accountability (ALLEA, 2017, p. 4). Relating to others through research is profoundly ethical. From a posthuman point of view, the philosopher Rosi Braidotti (2018, p. 182) reminds us,

> [r]esearchers are neither the legislators, nor the showmen of contemporary culture, but are people involved in the production of knowledge and power, knowledge as power, in a fast-changing world. We owe allegiance to the world, to the present. Thinking of ourselves as becoming-nomads of science and the becoming-nomads of research is absolutely crucial.

Hence, human vigilance is in jeopardy no matter profession or position: 'Ironically, only those who understand their own potential for unethical behavior can become the ethical decision makers that they aspire to be', Banjani, Bazerman, and Chugh argue (2003, p. 9).

Thus, the *virtuous* music researcher treads gently, using her/his skills recognizable as wisdom, courage, moderation, and fairness, while striving to elucidate the music's potential in people's life—in a broad sense.

Performing respect in real-life encounters and research on music as a human condition emerges from situatedness while profoundly affecting the music professional's integrity.

## Summary

This chapter has addressed music and ethics in real-life music encounters exemplified through different roles at various arenas. The onset of the chapter inspected different perceptions of music as a phenomenon, before elaborating on the musical ethics relationship. After that, different roles and contexts were illustrated and explored through real-music encounters within various music practices:

- The musician: ethics in performance
- The music educator: ethics in teaching
- The music therapist: ethics in therapy
- The musicologist: ethics in theory-building
- The 'lay' musician: ethics in everyday musicking, and
- The music researcher: ethics in research.

The illustrative examples followed the same structure: elaborating on ethical problems, dilemmas, and unpleasant experiences, in addition to suggested strategies for ethical training of music students within various fields of music professionalism. The examples illustrated that problems, dilemmas, and unpleasant experiences might be similar but diverse to the different music roles, arenas, and contexts, in both the music and ethics encounters and in professional training.

As musical beings, we encounter the Other—in an ethical responsibility. Therefore, an encounter with the Other is an encounter with ourselves. Such a joint becoming, with the Other in-person or through memories, was exemplified through everyday musicking.

Musical engagement creates realities, from micro- to macro levels. The examples opened for exploring various crossroads between professional and personal musical ethics endeavour in the experience, material, and context. Hence, a 'musical-ethics-demand' faces diversities at a cultural, political, and ecological level. Such a musical ethics endeavour is also relational as individuality and sociality illuminate that control and freedom are at stake.

The next and final chapter connects and extends the music-philosophical discourse of music and ethics and the musical ethics' practical crossroads and influences, turning to reflexivity, hence an *ethical musicality*. Before discussing musicality, we offer a conceptual basis for ethical musicality. Furthermore, an ethical musicality unfolds, focusing on the body, relationship, time, and space, incorporating context, involvement, power, responsibility, sustainability, and hope. Hence, an ethical musicality—an art of becoming—offering hope of a 'good life'.

## References

Aalbers, S., Fusar-Poli, L., Freeman, R. E., Spreen, M., Ket, J. C. F., Vink, A. C., ... Gold, C. (2017). Music therapy for depression. *Cochrane Database of Systematic Reviews* (11). http://doi.org/10.1002/14651858.CD004517.pub3.
ALLEA. (2017). *The European code of conduct for research integrity*. Berlin: All European Academies (ALLEA). Retrieved from https://allea.org/code-of-conduct/.
Allsup, R. E., & Westerlund, H. (2012). Methods and situational ethics in music education. *Action, Criticism & Theory for Music Education*, *11*(1), 124–148.
Ansdell, G. (2014). *Where music helps in music therapy and everyday life*. Surrey: Ashgate.
Ansdell, G., & DeNora, T. (2016). *Musical pathways in recovery: Community music therapy and mental wellbeing*. Farnham: Ashgate.
Ansdell, G., & Stige, B. (2018). Can music therapy still be humanist? *Music Therapy Perspectives*, *36*, 175–168.
Baltazar, M., Västfjäll, D., & Asutay, E. (2019). Is it me or the music? Stress reduction and the role of regulation strategies and music. *Music & Science*, *2*, 1–16. http://doi.org/10.1177/2059204319844161.
Bandura, B. A. (1986). *Social foundation of thought and action. A social cognitive theory*. Englewood Cliff, NJ: Prentice-Hall Inc.
Banjani, M. R., Bazerman, M. H., & Chugh, D. (2003). How (un)ethical are you? *Harvard Business Review* (December), 1–9.
Barad, K. (2008). Posthumanist performativity: Toward an understanding of how matter comes to matter. In S. H. Stacy Alaimo (Ed.), *Material feminisms* (pp. 120–154). Bloomington: Indiana University Press.
Bartleet, B.-L., & Higgins, L. (Eds.). (2018). *The Oxford handbook of community music*. Oxford and New York: Oxford University Press.
Batt-Rawden, K. B., DeNora, T., & Ruud, E. (2005). Music listening and empowerment in health promotion: A study of the role and significance of music in everyday life of the long-term ill. *Nordic Journal of Music Therapy*, *14*(2), 120–136. http://doi.org/10.1080/08098130509478134.
Benestad, F. (1976). *Musikk og tanke. Hovedretninger i musikkestetikkens historie fra antikken til vår egen tid (Music and thought. Main directions in the history of music aesthetics from Antiquity to our time)*. Oslo: Aschehoug.
Blichfeldt-Ærø, S. C., Knutsen, T. M., Hagen, H. M., Diep, L. M., Trondalen, G., & Halvorsen, S. (2020). Music therapy as an adjunct in cardiac device lead extraction procedures: A randomized controlled trial. *Applied Nursing Research* (56) (December). doi:10.1016/j.apnr.2020.151376.
Bonde, L. O. (2009). *Musik og menneske. Introduktion til musikpsykologi (Music and the human being. Introduction to music psychology)*. Frederiksberg C: Samfundslitteratur.

Bonde, L. O., & Theorell, T. (Eds.). (2018). *Music and public health. A Nordic perspective*. Switzerland AG: Springer Nature.
Bordieu, P. (1998). *Practical reason. On the theory of action*. Cambridge: Stanford University Press.
Braidotti, R. (2018). Affirmative ethics, posthuman subjectivity, and intimate scholarship: A conversation with Rosi Braidotti. In *Decentering the researcher in intimate scholarship: Critical posthuman methodological perspectives in education (Advances in Research on Teaching)* (Vol. 31, pp. 179–188). Bingley: Emerald Publishing Limited. https://doi.org/10.1108/S1479-368720180000031014.
Brotons, M., Chan, V., Chong, H. J., Clements-Cortes, A., Leonard, H., Norris, M., . . . Zanini, C. (2022). Global perspectives on addressing systemic issues in music therapy curricula and healthcare. Paper presented at the 12th European Music Therapy Conference. Music Therapy in Progress, Please Disturb, Edinburgh, Scotland, June 9.
Bruya, B. J. (2008). Education and responsiveness. On the agency of intersubjectivity. In R. T. Ames & P. D. Hershock (Eds.), *Educations and their purposes* (pp. 346–353). Honolulu: University of Hawai'i Press.
Buller, J. (2002). What is it like to be an injured musician? *Canadian Music Educator, 43*(4), 20–23.
Carlsen, M., & Holm, H. (2017). *Å tolke musikk. (Interpreting music)*. Oslo: Universitetsforlaget.
Carlson, E., Wilson, J., Baltazar, M., Duman, D., Peltola, H.-R., Toiviainen, P., & Saarikallio, S. (2021). The role of music in everyday life during the first wave of the coronavirus pandemic: A mixed-methods exploratory study. *Frontiers in Psychology, 12*. http://doi.org/10.3389/fpsyg.2021.647756.
Carter, T. E., & Panisch, L. S. (2021). A systematic review of music therapy for psychosocial outcomes of substance use clients. *International Journal of Mental Health and Addiction*, 1551–1568. http://doi.org/10.1007/s11469-020-00246-8.
Cobussen, M., & Nielsen, N. (2012/2016). *Music and ethics*. London and New York: Routledge.
Cox, D., & Levine, M. (2016). Music and ethics: The very mildly interesting view. In *Oxford handbooks online* (February). https://doi.org/10.1093/oxfordhb/9780199935321.013.145
Decker-Vogt, H.-H. (2012). "Mich macht krank, was ich liebe" ("What I love makes me sick"). In H.-H. Decker-Vogt (Ed.), *Zwischen Tönen und Wörten. Ein Reader mit Aufsätzen, reden und Interviews (Between sounds and words. A reader of essays, speeches and interviews)* (pp. 67–112). Wiesbaden: Reichelt Verlag.
Declaration of Helsinki. (1964). Declaration of Helsinki. Retrieved from www.wma.net/policies-post/wma-declaration-of-helsinki-ethical-principles-for-medical-research-involving-human-subjects/.
DeNora, T. (2000). *Music in everyday life*. Cambridge: Cambridge University Press.
DeNora, T. (2013). *Music asylums. Wellbeing through music in everyday life*. Farnham and Burlington: Ashgate.
DeNora, T., & Ansdell, G. (2014). What can't music do? *Psychology of Well-Being, 4*(23). http://doi.org/10.1186/s13612-014-0023-6.
Dileo, C. (2021). *Ethical thinking in music therapy* (2nd ed.). Cherry Hill: Jeffrey Books.

Ethics as a practice 53

DiMaio, L., & Engen, B. (2020). Ethics in music therapy education. Four points to consider. *Music Therapy Perspectives*, *38*(1), 42–50. http://doi.org/10.1093/mtp/miz030.

dos Santos, A. (2020). The usefulness of aggression as explored by becoming-teenagers in group music therapy. *Nordic Journal of Music Therapy*, *29*(2), 150–173. https://doi.org/10.1080/08098131.2019.1649712.

Ekholm, O., Juel, K., & Bonde, L. O. (2016). Music and public health—An empirical study of the use of music in the daily life of the adult Danish citizens and the health implications of musical participation. *Arts & Health*, *8*(2), 154–168.

Elliot, D. J. (1991). Music as knowledge. *Philosophy of Music Education Newsletter*, *3*(2), 1–2. Retrieved from www.jstor.org/stable/25666144.

Erkkilä, J., Punkanen, M., Fachner, J., Ala-Ruona, E., Pöntiö, I., Tervaniemi, M., . . . Gold, C. (2011). Individual music therapy for depression: Randomised controlled trial. *British Journal of Psychiatry*, *199*(2), 132–139. http://doi.org/10.1192/bjp.bp.110.085431.

EU. (2018). General data protection regulations (GDPR), May 25. Retrieved from https://gdpr.eu/what-is-gdpr/.

Fachner, J. (2017). Retraining of drug reward, music cues and state-dependent recall in music therapy. *Music and Medicine*, *9*(1), 8–14. http://doi.org/10.47513/mmd.v9i1.524.

Farrant, C., Pavlicevic, M., & Tsiris, G. (2014). *A guide to research ethics for arts therapists and arts and health practitioners*. London and Philadelphia: Jessica Kingsley Publishers.

Finley, S. (2014). An introduction to critical arts-based research. Demonstrating methodologies and practices of a radical ethical aesthetic. *Cultural Studies ↔ Critical Methodologies (CSCM)*, *14*(6). http://doi.org/10.1177/1532708614548123.

Fuhr, G., & Stensæth, K. (2022). *Therapy–the problematic word in music therapy with adolescents in the child welfare services*. Voices. A World Forum for Music Therapy 22(3). https://doi.org/https://doi.org/10.15845/voices.v22i3.3380.

Gabrielson, A. (2011). *Strong experiences with music. Music is much more than just music*. Oxford: Oxford University Press.

Ghetti, C., Chen, X.-J., Brenner, A. K., Hakvoort, L. G., Lien, L., Fachner, J., & Gold, C. (2022). Music therapy for people with substance use disorders. *Cochrane Database of Systematic Reviews*. https://doi.org/10.1002/14651858.CD012576.pub3.

Glaser, B. G., & Strauss, A. L. (1967). *The discovery of grounded theory. Strategies for qualitative research*. New York: Aldine de Gruyter.

Gold, C., Mössler, K., Grocke, D., Heldal, T. O., Tjemsland, L., Aarre, T., . . . Rolvsjord, R. (2013). Individual music therapy for mental health care clients with low therapy motivation: Multicentre randomised controlled trial. *Psychotherapy and Psychosomatics*, *82*(5), 319–331. http://doi.org/10.1159/000348452.

Griffith-Dickson, G. (2012). Teaching philosophy of religion "multiculturally". A Lōkahi approach. In R. T. Ames & P. D. Hershock (Eds.), *Educations and their purposes* (pp. 72–90). Honolulu: University of Hawai'i Press.

Hatfield, J. L. (2016). Performing at the top of one's musical game. *Frontiers in Psychology*, *7*. http://doi.org/10.3389/fpsyg.2016.01356.

## 54  Ethics as a practice

Higgins, K. M. (2011). *The music of our lives*. Lanham, Boulder, New York, Toronto and Plymouth, UK: Lexington Books.

Higgins, K. M. (2018). Connecting music to ethics. *College Music Symposium: Journal of the College Music Society, 58*(3). http://doi.org/10.18177/sym.2018.58.sr.11411.

Hines, M., & McFerran, K. (2014). Metal made me who I am. Seven adult men reflect on their engagement with metal music during adolescence. *International Journal of Community Music, 7*(2), 205–222. http://doi.org/10.1386/ijcm.7.2.205_1.

Hjellbrekke, J., Drivdal, L., Ingierd, H., Rekdal, O. B., Skramstad, H., Torp, I. S., & Kaiser, M. (2018). Research integrity in Norway–results from a nationwide survey on research ethics. Retrieved from www.forskningsetikk.no/globalassets/dokumenter/4-publikasjoner-som-pdf/rino-report-no-1—research-integrity-in-norway—results-from-a-nationwide-survey-on-research-ethics.pdf.

Horden, P. (Ed.). (2000). *Music as medicine. The history of music therapy since Antiquity*. Aldershot, Burlington USA, Singapore and Sidney: Ashgate.

Johannesen, K. I., Molven, O., & Roalkvam (Eds.). (2007). *Godt, rett, rettferdig. Etikk for sykepleiere (Good, right, fair. Ethics for nurses)*. Oslo: Akribe.

Johansen, G. (2021). The hidden curriculum in higher music education. In R. Wright, G. Johansen, P. A. Kanellopoulos, & P. Schmidt (Eds.), *The Routledge handbook to sociology of music education*. London: Routledge.

Johansson, Y. L. (2010). *Psykosocial arbetsmiljö i en yrkesgrupp med krav på hög kvalitet—orkestrar innom kunstmusik (Psychosocial work environment in a profession aspiring at excellency—professional orchestras)*. (PhD). Karolinska Institutet, Stockholm, Sweden.

Jourdan, K. (2012). Towards an ethical music education? Looking through the lens of Levinas. *Music Education Research, 14*(3), 381–399. doi:10.1080/14613808.2012.699956.

Karlsen, S. (2011). Using musical agency as a lens. Researching music education from the angle of experience. *Research Studies in Music Education, 33*(2), 107–121. http://doi.org/10.1177/1321103X11422005.

Kildahl, K. (Ed.). (2020). *Skikket for yrket? Skikkethetsvurdering i profesjonsutdanninger (Suited for the profession? Aptitude assessment in professional education)*. Oslo: Universitetsforlaget.

Kim, C. (2004). Nurturing students through group lessons. *American Music Teacher, 54*(1), 28–31.

Kjerschow, P. C. (1978/91). *Musikk og mening (Music and meaning)*. Oslo: Idé og tanke.

Kosteletos, G., & Georgaki, A. (2014). From digital 'echos' to virtual 'ethos': Ethical aspects of music technology. *Psychology, Computer Science*, 193–200. http://doi.org/10.5281/ZENODO.850500.

Krüger, V. (2020). *Music therapy in child welfare. Bridging provision, protection and participation*. Dallas, TX: Barcelona Publishers.

Kruse, B. (2016). *Thinking art. An interdisciplinary approach to applied aesthetics* (Vol. 2, NMH-Publications). Oslo: Norwegian Academy of Music.

Lévinas, E. (1991/1998). *Entre nous. Thinking-of-the-other* (M. B. Smith & B. Harshav, Trans. L. D. Kritzman, Ed.). New York: Colombia University Press.

Lincoln, Y. S., & Guba, E. G. (1985). *Naturalistic inquiry*. London, UK: Sage.
Lines, D. (2018). The ethics of community music In B.-L. Bartleet & L. Higgins (Eds.), *The Oxford handbook of community music*. Oxford and New York: Oxford University Press.
Løgstrup, K. E. (1956/1997). *The ethical demand* (T. I. Jensen, G. Puckering, & E. Watkins, Trans.). Notre Dame and London: University of Notre Dame Press.
MacDonald, R., Hargreaves, D. J., & Miell, D. (Eds.). (2017). *Handbook of musical identities*. Oxford: Oxford University Press.
MacDonald, R., Kreutz, G., & Mitchell, L. (2012). *Music, health, wellbeing*. Oxford: Oxford University Press.
McAuley, T., Nielsen, N., Levinson, J., & Phillips-Hutton, A. (Eds.). (2021). *Western music and philosophy*. Oxford: Oxford University Press.
McClary, S. K. (2002). *Feminist endings: Music, gender, and sexuality* (2nd ed.). Minneapolis: University of Minnesota Press.
McFerran, K. S. (2011a, October 26). Exclusive: Dr. Katrina McFerran responds to reaction towards her study on music and mood. Retrieved from https://metalinsider.net/guest-blog/exclusive-dr-katrina-mcferran-responds-to-reaction-towards-her-study-on-music-and-mood.
McFerran, K. S. (2011b). Music therapy with bereaved youth: Expressing grief and feeling better. *Prevention Researcher*, *18*(3), 17–20.
McFerran, K. S. (2016). Contextualising the relationship between music, emotions and the well-being of young people: A critical interpretive synthesis. *Musicae Scientiae*, *20*(1), 103–121. http://doi.org/10.1177/1029864915626968.
McFerran, K. S., Garrido, S., & Saarikallio, S. (2013). A critical interpretive synthesis of the literature linking music and adolescent depression. *Youth and Society*, *48*(4), 521–538. http://doi.org/10.1177/0044118X13501343.
Merleau-Ponty, M. (1945/89). *Phenomenology and perception*. London: Routledge.
Meyer, L. B. (1956). *Emotion and meaning in music*. Chicago: University of Chicago Press.
Middelstadt, S. E., & Fishbein, M. (1988). Health and occupational correlates of perceived occupational stress in symphony orchestra musicians. *Journal of Occupational Medicine*, *30*(9), 687–692.
Moland, A. (2021). *Det skjulte nettverket. Farlige forbindler mellom unge på nettet (The hidden network. Dangerous connections between young people online)*. Oslo: Cappelen Damm.
Moore, S. K. (2013). A systematic review on the neural effects of music on emotion regulation: Implications for music therapy practice. *Journal of Music Therapy*, *50*(3), 198–242. http://doi.org/10.1093/jmt/50.3.198.
Navone, S., & Carollo, G. (2016). Extremely fragile: Playing with care! A study on music therapy's application with young patients suffering from drug addiction. *Nordic Journal of Music Therapy*, *25*(1 suppl. 1), 52–53. doi:10.1080/08098131.2016.1179962.
Nielsen, S. G., & Dyndahl, P. (2021). Music education, genderfication, and symbolic violence. In R. Wright, G. Johansen, P. A. Kanellopoulos, & P. Schmidt (Eds.), *The Routledge handbook to sociology of music education*. London: Routledge.

Nielsen, S. G., Johansen, G. G., & Jørgensen, H. (2018). Peer learning in instrumental practicing. *Frontiers in Psychology*, *9*. http://doi.org/10.3389/fpsyg.2018.00339.

Nissen-Lie, H. A., Monsen, J. T., & Rønnestad, M. H. (2010). Therapist predictors of early patient-rated working alliance: A multilevel approach. *Psychotherapy Research*, *20*(6), 627–646. http://doi.org/10.1080/10503307.2010.497633.

Nussbaum, M. C. (2003). *Upheavals of thought: The intelligence of emotions*. Chicago, IL: University of Chicago Press.

Nussbaum, M. C. (2011). *Creating capabilities. The human development approach*. Cambridge, MA: The Belknap Press of Harvard University Press.

OECD. (2020). Culture shock: COVID-19 and the cultural and creative sectors. Retrieved from The Organization for Economic Cooperation and Development. www.oecd.org/coronavirus/policy-responses/culture-shock-covid-19-and-the-cultural-and-creative-sectors-08da9e0e/#section-d1e44.

Pedersen, I. N., Lindvang, C., & Beck, B. D. (Eds.). (2022). *Resonant learning in music therapy. A training model to tune the therapist*. London and Philadelphia: Jessica Kingsley Publishers.

Phillips-Hutton, A., & Nielsen, N. (2021). Ethics. In T. Mcauley, N. Nielsen, J. Levinson, & A. Phillips-Hutton (Eds.), *The Oxford handbook of Western music and philosophy* (pp. 283–306). Oxford: Oxford University Press.

Pool, J., & Odell-Miller, H. (2011). Aggression in music therapy and its role in creativity with reference to personality disorder. *The Arts in Psychotherapy*, *38*, 169–177.

Rinde, F. B., & Christophersen, C. (2021). Developing an understanding of intercultural music education in a Nordic setting. *Nordic Research in Music Education*, *2*(2), 5–27. http://doi.org/10.23865/nrme.v2.2772.

Robson, C. (1993/2002). *Real world research. A resource for social scientists and practitioner-researchers* (2nd ed.). Oxford: Blackwell Publishers.

Rolvsjord, R. (2015). What clients do to make music therapy work. A qualitative multiple case study in adult mental health care. *Nordic Journal of Music Therapy*, *24*(4), 296–321. http://doi.org/10.1080/08098131.2014.964753.

Røyseng, S., Henningsen, E., & Vinge, J. (2022). The moral outlooks of cultural workers in pandemic times. *Nordisk kulturpolitisk tidsskrift*, *25*(2). doi:10.18261/nkt.25.2.3.

Ruud, E. (2013). Music, grief and life crisis. In L. O. Bonde, E. Ruud, M. S. Skånland, & G. Trondalen (Eds.), *Musical life stories. Narratives on health musicking* (Vol. 5, NMH-Publications, pp. 165–180). Oslo: CREMAH, Norges musikkhøgskole.

Ruud, E. (2016). *Musikkvitenskap (Musicology)*. Oslo: Universitetsforlaget.

Ruud, E. (2020). *Towards a sociology of music therapy: Musicking as a cultural immunogen*. Dallas, TX: Barcelona Publishers.

Salimpoor, V. N., Benovoy, M., Larcher, K., Dagher, A., & Zatorre, R. J. (2011). Anatomically distinct dopamine release during anticipation and experience of peak emotion to music. *Nature Neuroscience*, *14*(2), 257–262. doi:10.1038/nn.2726.

Schäfer, K., Saarikallio, S., & Eerola, T. (2020). Music may reduce loneliness and act as social surrogate for a friend: Evidence from an experimental listening study. *Music & Science*, *3*, 1–16. http://doi.org/10.1177/2059204320935709.

Short, A. D. L., & Dingle, G. A. (2015). Music as an auditory cue for emotions and cravings in adults with substance use disorders. *Psychology of Music, 44*(3), 559–573.

Skånland, M. S. (2012). *A technology of well-being. A qualitative study on the use of MP3 players as a medium for musical self-care*. London: Lambert Academic Publishing.

Skårderud, F. (2003). Shame in cyberspace. Relationships without faces: The e-media and eating disorders. *European Eating Disorders Review, 11*(3), 155–169.

Slotfeldt-Ellingsen, D. (2020). *Forskningsetikk. Yrkesetikk ved forskningsvirksomhet (Research ethics. Professional ethics in research)*. Oslo: Universitetsforlaget.

Small, C. (1998). *Musicking. The meanings of performing and listening*. Hanover: University Press of New England.

Solli, H. P., & Rolvsjord, R. (2015). "The opposite of treatment": A qualitative study of how patients diagnosed with psychosis experience music therapy. *Nordic Journal of Music Therapy, 24*(1), 67–92. http://doi.org/10.1080/08098131.2014.890639.

Stegemann, T., & Weymann, E. (2019). *Ethik in der Musiktherapie. Grundlagen und Praxis (Ethics in music therapy. Foundation and practice)*. Giessen: Psychosozial-Verlag.

Stige, B., Malterud, K., & Midtgarden, T. (2009). Toward an agenda for evaluation of qualitative research. *Qualitative Health Research, 19*(10), 1504–1516. doi:10.1177/1049732309348501.

Taborsky, C. (2007). Musical performance anxiety: A review of literature. *UPDATE-Applications of Research in Music Education, 26*(1) (Fall–Winter), 15–25.

Teitelbaum, B. (2014). "The path of dreams": Breivik, music, and-neo-nazi skinheadism. In J. S. Knudsen, M. S. Skånland, & G. Trondalen (Eds.), *Musikk etter 22. juli (Music after the 22nd of July)* (Vol. 5, NMH-publikasjoner, pp. 119–138). Oslo: CREAMH, Norges musikkhøgskole.

Teixeira, W., & Ferraz, S. (2018). Musical performance ethics. *Debates in UNIRIO*(20), 27–47. Retrieved from www.academia.edu/36865803/Musical_Performance_Ethics.

Thom, P. (2021). Performance. In T. Mcauley, N. Nielsen, J. Levinson, & A. Phillips-Hutton (Eds.), *The Oxford handbook of Western music and philosophy* (pp. 467–482). Oxford: Oxford University Press.

Thomassen, M. (2019). Menneskets menneskelighet. Frihet og ansvar i Emmanuel Lévinas filosofi (Human humanity. Freedom and responsibility in Emmanuel Lévinas' philosophy). *SEGL—Katolsk Årsskrift for Religion og Samfunn*, 103–111.

Torp, I. S. (2017). Uredelig forskning lever videre (Fraudulent research lives on). *Forskningsetikk* (1), 4–6.

Trondalen, G. (2013). Musical performance as health promotion: A musician's narrative. In L. O. Bonde, M. S. Skånland, E. Ruud, & G. Trondalen (Eds.), *Musical life stories. Narratives on health musicking* (Vol. 6, NMH-Publications, pp. 181–200). Oslo: CREMAH, Norwegian Academy of Music.

Trondalen, G. (2016a). *Relational music therapy. An intersubjective perspective*. Dallas, TX: Barcelona Publishers.

Trondalen, G. (2016b). Resource-oriented Bonny method og Guided Imagery and Music (R-oGIM) as a health resource for musicians. *Nordic Journal of Music Therapy, 25*(1), 5–31. http://doi.org/10.1080/08098131.2014.987804.

## 58 Ethics as a practice

Trondalen, G. (2021). Når klær blir etikk. Om knytebluser, virkeligheter og formative visjoner. (When clothes become ethics. On tie blouses, realities and formative visions). *Musikkterapi, 24*(1), 34–37.

Trondalen, G., & Wosch, T. (2016). Microanalysis in interpretivist research. In B. Wheeler & K. Murphy (Eds.), *Music therapy research* (3rd ed., Chapter 55). Dallas, TX: Barcelona Publishers.

UN. (1948). United nations, universal declaration of human rights (UDHR). Retrieved from www.un.org/en/about-us/universal-declaration-of-human-rights.

UN. (2015). United nations, sustainable development goals, agenda 2030. Retrieved from www.undp.org/sustainable-development-goals.

Valberg, T. (2011). *En relasjonell musikkestetikk. Barn på orkesterselskapenes konserter (A relational aesthetics of music–children at professional orchestras' concerts)*. (Doctoral dissertation). Göteborg Universitet, Sweden.

Valberg, T. (2014). Kan barn oppleve kunst? (Are children able to experience art?). *Kulturrådet*. Retrieved from www.kulturradet.no/kunstloftet/vis-artikkel/-/kl-artikkel-2014-musikkviter-tony-valberg.

Vancouver, Recommendations. (1979). Vancouver recommendations. Retrieved from www.icmje.org/icmje-recommendations.pdf.

Viega, M. (2016). Science as art: Axiology as a central component in methodology and evaluation of arts-based research. *Music Therapy Perspectives, 34*(1). http://doi.org/10.1093/mtp/miv043.

Vinter, T., Enebakk, V., & Hølen, C. J. (Eds.). (2016). *Vitenskapelig (u)redelighet (Scientific (dis)honesty)*. Oslo: Cappelen Damm AS.

Vist, T., & Bonde, L. O. (2013). "Then certain songs came": Music listening in the grieving process after losing a child. In L. O. Bonde, E. Ruud, M. S. Skånland, & G. Trondalen (Eds.), *Musical life stories: Narratives on health musicking* (Vol. 5, NMH-Publications, pp. 139–163). Oslo: CREMAH, Norges musikkhøgskole.

Vuoskoski, J. K., Zickfeld, J. H., Alluri, V., Moorthigari, V., & Seibt, B. (2022). Feeling moved by music: Investigating continuous ratings and acoustic correlates. *Plus One*. http://doi.org/10.1371/journal.pone.0261151.

Warren, J. R. (2014). *Music and ethical responsibility*. Cambridge: Cambridge University Press.

Westerlund, H., Karslen, S., & Kallio, A. (2021). Professional reflexivity and the paradox of freedom. Negotiating professional boundaries in a Jewish Ultra-Orthodox female music teacher education programme. *International Journal of Music Education, 39*(4), 424–437. http://doi.org/10.1177/0255761421988924.

Williamon, A. (2004). *Music excellence. Strategies and techniques to enhance performance*. Oxford: Oxford University Press.

# 3 Reflexivity
## Music and ethics

This chapter combines and extends a music-philosophical discourse of music and ethics and musical ethics' practical crossroads. It aspires to reflexivity, hence an *ethical musicality*. The introduction elaborates on ethical musicality as a concept before reflecting on cultures of musicality. The section 'toward an ethical musicality' is divided into five parts. The first two segments of ethical musicality focus on the body, relationship, time, and space. Following these fundamental existentials, the chapter expands our lifeworld, embracing context, involvement, power, responsibility, sustainability, and hope. Hence, an ethical musicality—an art of becoming—offering hope of a 'good life'.

But what is 'ethical musicality'? Ethical musicality is a shaping of thoughts and ideas merged into a *conceptual framework*—with existential implications. Ruud (2020, p. 17) argues in line with Deleuze and Guattari (1991/1994),

> [a] concept is not to be reduced to a specific meaning of the word; instead, it is a complex structure to which it is not that easy to give a dictionary definition. A concept is a way of organizing information that would otherwise remain chaotic, showing through the concept how the same chaos can be ordered in a different way.

Ethical musicality creates new ways of approaching and dealing with the linkage between music and ethics, people and culture, individuality and sociality, and ecology. It is not a given entity but an invention of prevailing and emergent ideas—in becoming. Thinking conceptually about ethical musicality comprehends a transfer from a philosophical-theoretical level to real-life experiences and vice versa. Hence, the forthcoming sections elucidate an ethical musicality with lived implications.

## Cultures of musicality

The concept of ethical musicality implies ethics, developed relatively thoroughly so far in the text. It also draws on *musicality*, which unfolds in the following paragraph focusing on

- communicative musicality
- musicianship, and
- culture

while eventually suggesting musicality as a *lived experience*.

In *Communicative musicality*, Malloch and Trevarthen (2009a) explore the intrinsic musical nature of human interaction. The infant's interaction with other people is rooted in an innate differentiation system (Trevarthen, 1999). In other words, this mutual exchange is universal and not learned. Such an assessment takes place, among other things, with reference to Bateson's term proto-conversation (1975) and Papousêk and Papousêk's word 'musicality' (1981). Malloch and Trevarthen (2009b) clarify their use of 'musicality' and 'musical', referring to 'musicality' as 'innate human abilities', allowing for music appreciation and production. They say:

> We define musicality as expression of our human desire for cultural learning, our innate skill for moving, remembering and planning in sympathy with others that make our appreciation and production of an endless variety of dramatic temporal narratives possible.
>
> (p. 4)

Communicative musicality, then, is an innate psycho-biological *capacity*. Microanalysis of a musical relationship shows how our innate ability allows for 'dramatic temporal narratives' played out through gaze, tone of voice, movements, tempo, intensity, timing, and regulation of proximity and distance. These forms are *musical dynamics* of *lived relationship experiences* over time (Johns, 2018). Musical dynamics convey rhythm and intensity, resonating with expressive and receptive modes of experiencing music, promoting the feeling of being alive.

An interesting question emerges: *can* musicality as an inborn (pre-active) capacity be ethical? At first glance, probably not. But what if we twist the question? Communicative musicality promotes the feeling of being alive. Might being left alone in one's capacity mean existential loneliness and eventually psycho-biological 'death' of the intrinsic musical nature of human communication? From a philosophical perspective, such a 'locked up' musicality connects ethics and our *shared human ground*. Maybe re-visiting a complex and detailed micro-analysis of musical dynamics of lived relationship experiences can shed light upon and direct ethical reflection towards our common human *capacities*? Can re-viewing the crucial influence of a musical capacity, which potentially allows for the sharing of lifeworlds, support ethical reflection on our shared human *vulnerability*? A new question arises: how do we move from communicative musicality towards skilled musicianship in a cultural context? Is it possible to move back and forth between musicality as an inborn capacity and collaborative musicking in a musical community?

Pavlicevic and Andsdell (2009) engage in such a possible link between musicality as a capacity and collaborative musicing (sic., p. 358). They argue that the theory of communicative musicality provides a necessary but insufficient theoretical platform to elaborate on social and cultural levels of musicing. How then to move from the close and intimate musicality (an innate capacity) articulated as a two-some 'dance of well-being' (Trevarthen & Malloch, 2000) towards professional musician's performances and collaborative musicking in the community? The authors propose a model where 'the relationship between musical and social experiences generates and is generated by musical communication and musical collaboration' (Pavlicevic & Andsdell, 2009, p. 364).

In our opinion, the authors point to an essential, often overlooked, argument. As caregivers and infants use their capacity to communicate (a dyadic form of relatedness) through diverse *musical dynamics*, the mother or father will always bring elements from their musical culture into the proto- and turn-taking communication, such as lullabies (Bonnár, 2014) and nursery rhymes. These utterances with cultural bearings affect the dyadic procedural communication at a local level, leading to a 'we' *in* culture. Pavlicevic and Andsdell (2009, p. 364) say

> [A]s the dyad takes in elements of musical culture (e.g., in mother's vocalizations and nursery songs)—communication begins to service the development of musicianship (the expression of musicality in and as culture).... When we reach 'We', a genuine musical partnership has been built on the platform of communicative musicality and the ongoing cultural induction of musicianship.

We might argue that the infant already, from the start, experiences a supposed 'we', a primary intersubjectivity (Trevarthen, 1980). However, the point here is to accentuate the awareness of a musical *cultural* 'we'.

From the dyad-musicianship, Pavlicevic and Andsdell (2009) suggest a further function, which is not only communicative but also collaborative. They call this music/sociality relationship 'collaborative musicing' (p. 364).

Such a collaborative musicing 'builds community through making music together', in other words, collaborative musicing is scaffolded by musical communication. However, the authors accentuate that it is not solely the accumulation of the dyadic musical communication, but the 'facilitation of paradyadic musical experiences' that makes collaborative musicing possible (pp. 364–365). They distinguish between these related but separately identifiable lived concepts of communication and collaboration. Additionally, they emphasize that we are in an in-between position oscillating between the modes of communication and collaboration due to our various fundamental existentials (I/you/we/us) and lived performances (musicality/musicianship/musicing).

Following our explorative approach to the phenomenon of musicality, we need to address musicality as a pre-condition for *musicianship*. The underlying basis of musicianship is 'a cultivated faculty of musicality-in-action within sociocultural contexts' (Pavlicevic & Andsdell, 2009, p. 262). It includes questions such as innate talent, skills, techniques, strategies, physical and mental demands, education, and musical excellence to enhance performance (Jørgensen & Lehmann, 1997; Nielsen et al., 2018; Williamon, 2004). Cultivation and hard work are evidently vital parts of such a musicianship.

We appreciate the term musicality, which is used for some people, who seem to be more musically gifted or talented in their cultural learning than others, that is, inhabiting a significant potential for cultivating and performing various music in their musicianship. Such a matter of aptitude is similar to other professions, such as excellency in sports (Hatfield & Lemyre, 2016). However, the implication of such a view on musicality also relates to economic and social affordances. Developing skills on an instrument may relate to social capital (Bordieu, 1998), gentrification (Dyndahl et al., 2020), and (dis)advantaged environments. Musicianship and, hence, musicality, becomes a matter of ethics.

Ethical musicality does not counteract cultivated musicianship. However, it embraces all people's musicality affordances and appropriations as well. Where does this lead us? As ethical musicality emerges in proximity to people, contexts, and cultures, maybe we can discuss an interdisciplinary understanding of *cultures of musicality?* Perhaps an ethical musicality can approach cultures of musicality by elaborating on what is and what constitutes culture?

In a dialogue on culture, cognitive psychologist Jerome Bruner and psychoanalyst Daniel Stern investigated constitutions of mind and cultures (Kallevik, 2007). Bruner (1990) elucidated how our minds constitute and are constituted by culture. He said we need to understand that all culture has narratives and that even in the most extraordinary things we do, the *ordinary* exposes. Stern (2004) dived from the grand notion of culture into the little, compact world of micro-culture, arguing whatever people do, they form a culture. He focused on what happens in the intersubjective field when a caregiver and her/his infant share a joint experience here and now. And by stretching themselves a step further together, they acquire new insight. How much is needed before a culture is constituted? A micro-dyad constitutes a culture, as do societal structures. There is a dialectic between the constitution of culture at micro- and macro levels.

Transferring the idea of micro- and macro cultures to an ethical musicality might offer an exceeding conception of musicality. Between the individual communicative musicality (capacity) with cultural utterances and the structurally constituted cultural musicality (musicianship), there must be a translation, as the *ordinary reveals in its specialty*. Every dyad of communicative musicality is 'ordinary', emerging from a capacity towards being shaped through cultural utterances of music. When being exposed to the social culture, the ordinary arises and prevails. Even when a musician does something that is not normal, such as *the* most spectacular performance on a world scene, the ordinary reveals through such as gaze, tone of voice, movements, tempo, intensity, timing, and regulation of proximity and distance. Hence, even in the extraordinary musicianship, the ordinary dynamic forms of musical lived experiences reveal.

It seems we can talk about *epistemology of musicality*, as various cultures have narratives of what constitutes musicality. We suggest the epistemology of musicality is parallel to the epistemology of music. With reference to ethnomusicology Cross and Tolbert (2021, p. 272) point to music as non-explicit,

> People in a culture know how to act and interact musically. Music has a social ontology, seems to be about subjectivity and intention, and models and is about social interaction.

Maybe the same counts for musicality; musicality exposes subjectivity and intention—and models the ordinary in sociality? We suggest such an epistemology of musicality may link to a capacity at a micro-level, cultivated via caregivers into a local musical culture.

Within an ethical musicality, musicality constitutes an exceeding category. We suggest that musicality is an existential dimension of seizing, absorbing, and participating in various modes of embodied musical experiences. Hence, musicality is not an intellectual constitution but a *lived experience*.

## Towards an ethical musicality

### Body and relationship

As human beings, we experience the world through our senses and bodies. Two philosophical views on how the body expresses the relationship between the individual and the surroundings became prevalent during the 20th century. These were the bodily and linguistic turns, which describe the relationship between the subject and the world to ontological and epistemological positions, respectively. The bodily turn links to phenomenology and hermeneutics, as the bodily subject establishes itself through its contact with the world. The body is seen as a *carrier* of subjectivity as it emerges and creates in sociality. Correspondingly, the linguistic turn is associated with social constructivism and discourse analysis. The relationship between the body and the world is then linguistically formed; hence language *produces* subjectivity (Holgersen, 2006).

The *lived body* refers to a phenomenological perception as we experience the body from an inside perspective. Also, we are sharing the world from an outside perspective. We experience the lifeworld and others through our intentional being. And as such, the body perceives and grasps simultaneously (Merleau-Ponty, 1945/89). The human being is one whole, capable of perception, expression, and memory. We are intersubjectively available to each other. We are relational. The phenomenal subjective body emerges in the here and now and is open to others through its intentional being. Additionally, there is a need for contextualization and interpretation in the musical presence when related to ethics, namely, *musical experience as lived*. Then, a basic premise is that bodily meaning does not emerge into only one essence—as meaning is multilayered.

Another position with ethical implications is the notion of musicality as an exceeding category, a lived experience. The human body exposes to musicality through its ability to seize, absorb, and participate in various modes of musical experiences. Such an existential position embraces communicate musicality. Hence, an inborn capacity facilitating development through intimate musical dynamics in a caregiver-infant relationship cultivated towards local musical culture (Pavlicevic & Andsdell, 2009). Such an experience with close others comes with an ethical call. Not in a Kantian sense, linked to morality and 'art for art's sake' (Benestad, 1976), but a call for an aesthetic opportunity. That is a value-based approach embracing musical sociality and community no matter age, musical skills, genre, or contextual setting.

One example previously mentioned is the children participating in a concert within the Western fine art setting. Such a *relational aesthetic* of music elucidates a new understanding of 'the child's rich perceptual state of readiness when listening to music', emerging through the relational matrix of intersubjectivity (Valberg, 2011). Intersubjectivity is an individual capacity (Trevarthen, 1980) *and* a field (Tronick, 1998). Innovative ways of being with each other unfold in the art room through new fragments of meaning (bodily and discursive) that further develop the children's narrative and, accordingly, their identity (Valberg, 2011).

The body has a phenomenological position in the world. Experiencing a body-related awareness in and through music might influence our senses of being in the world. That is, encountering various forms of musical engagement may eventually facilitate facets of the music's ethical capacity (Higgins, 2011; Phillips-Hutton & Nielsen, 2021). At a practical level, it might be a musical sound, intensity, or movement, embracing the body's inherent vulnerability, intentionality and not least, vitality. The musical dynamic forms of vitality connect to the experience of being alive. These inner forms of being alive are always open to intersubjective relatedness (Stern, 2010), not least through musicking (Trondalen, 2019a). Musical dynamics, then, is a concept describing lived relationship experiences over time (Johns, 2018). Accordingly, meaning emerges at a bodily, non-verbal level through and in music in the present, without necessary mentalization or communication afterwards.

The musical experience may also include value-based images, such as feelings, memories, spiritual experiences, symbols, and myths. These inner experiences of human significance and understanding, namely, presentational symbols (Langer, 1942/1974), offer meaning at an immediate level. An imagery component emerges and provides a sense of meaning without a consciously reflecting meaning-making process. Langer's validation of the music offering a vital symbolic transformation experience includes various ethically loaded values, embracing the whole lived experience as embodied.

Also, Stern refers to Langer's 'forms of feelings' (Langer, 1953/1973), acknowledging her focus on the music's many ways of describing feelings evoked by music, for example, 'fading, exulting, easiness, rushing' (Stern, 2010, p. 37). These categories do not necessarily belong to a specific act or action. Stern elaborates on dynamic forms of vitality, these inner dynamics of being alive, observable in musical interplay at a micro-level. Hence, music allows for meaning at a non-discursive level, valuing lived bodily experiences as ethically acceptable parts of a 'good life'.

Putting words to inner musical experiences involves cognitive processes, which remove us from experience per se. The tension between the immediate (bodily, non-discursive) level and the mediate (linguistic) level of experience is always present. We may share a joint, however, not an identical musical experience. But even if some *can* share an inner musical experience in words, language will always 'drive a wedge' (Stern, 2000, p. 162) between the experience as felt and the experience as narrated.

By offering value to non-discursive *and* discursive levels of music (Langer, 1942/1974; Stern, 2000), the ethical basis of music expands to recognizing experiences in a person's wholeness as the unique creation s/he is (Lévinas, 1961/2012). From an ethical point of view, opening oneself to a relating experience through music involves an act of trust (Løgstrup, 1956/1997; Trondalen, 2016a). In real-life musicking, the ethical demand fulfils at a personal and social level, as 'A person never has something to do with another person without also having some degree of control over him or her' (Løgstrup, 1956/1997, pp. 15–16). Following a musical experience as lived, control and freedom are also at stake in an ethical musicality.

Various philosophical entrances and ethical consideration have implications for the living body at a practical level. For example, technology connects to the living body and its relationship to the world, bringing ethical considerations. From a music performer's perspective with an artistic goal, a gestural voice processing instrument called 'The Throat' may elucidate (Elblaus et al., 2012). It is an artistically directed prototype where the lived relational musical body initiates vocal sounds. The performer engages with the musical performance and the perception of both the process and technological performance. An interesting issue is how artistic vision through practice might recontextualize technology and, without rebuilding it, redefine it and give it a new role. Various influences impact the technological developers, the musical performer and her/his musicianship, the performance, and the audience. 'The participants are therefore more than generic users—instead, they shape the role of the artifact (sic.) by using it in their own artistic process' (Elblaus et al., 2012, p. 383). Hence, the performing musician influences the creation of technology and performance from a relational bodily position while maintaining essential values in her/his life.

Yet another aspect links to the perception of—and appearances of—our lived bodies in the world, hence performativity. From a discursive perspective, we may ask, in line with the philosopher and gender theorist Judith Butler (1993; Jegerstedt, 2008), whether the traditional form of feminism has helped maintain—yes, even—reproduce the dominant ideology of gender as a hetero-normative regime? When Butler argues that biological gender is a 'doing' and not a 'being', a performative category, there will be consequences for both gender and sexual identity. Her point is that biology is not detached from discursive practice. Accordingly, discourses create realities; open and hidden values are in play through body and relationship.

## Time and space

The two following modalities focus on lived time and lived space. They are both existentials belonging to the human experience of being. The two dimensions refer to lived space as felt and lived time as our subjective and temporal way of being in the world. van. Manen suggests that 'The temporal dimensions of past, present, and future constitute the horizon of a person's landscape' (1990, p. 104). A moment, for example, has a dual presence. First, it happens in a present instant of chronos (clock time), while also unfolding in kairos (subjective time). Kairos is vital in the experience of music, as it solely connects to the subjective experience of 'felt time'. Such a way of perceiving and grasping time appreciates the human being per se, no matter mental, physical, or social position in life (Langer, 1953/1973). The art researcher Aldridge (1996, p. 37) says, 'In this conceptualization, time is in a state of flux; it is concerned with flexibility and the convergence of multiple tasks. Time is seen as springing from the self'.

Stern (2004, p. 58) elaborates on the present moment as a lived story. It has an emotional story line rather than being cognitively constructed. He argues that this is a special kind of story as 'it is lived as it happens'. These present moments, lived stories, are 'experiences that are narratively formatted in the mind but not verbalized or told' (p. 55). The temporal dimension of such a lived story is similar to a musical phase. Inspired by the phenomenologist Husserl (Føllesdal, 1993), Stern (2004) suggests that the present moment constitutes by a moment-to-moment experience. The past is present as an immediate memory (retention), while the future-of-the-present-moment is experienced as protension. The music unfolds simultaneously in chronos (objective measured time) and kairos (subjective experience). It involves a temporal quality both in the unfolding music and in the listener or performer of music (Ferrara, 1991).

As human beings, we are temporal and embodied beings within time and space. Engaging with music happens in a time-space continuum. With reference to phenomenology and neuroscience, Christensen (2012) suggests the basic music listening dimensions, intensity, timbre, movement, and pulse while the secondary dimensions constitute melody, rhythm, harmony, and micro-modulation. He then proposes that music listening integrates sensations of time and space in the experience of a virtual timespace.

From a similar position, neuroscience, and psychology, Wittmann (2017, p. xii) informs,

> [T]emporal experience depends on emotional and bodily states. . . . [B]odily sense, emotions, and the sense of time are all closely tied to the activities of a structure in the brain, the insular cortex.

The modality of time connects to various existential components. The dimension of time 'is inseparably tied to our experience as a whole, to our self-consciousness—to life itself. We are time' (p. xiii). Time and space link to our existence and are therefore of ethical importance.

Both present moments of short duration and longer musical phrases or songs/compositions connect to ethical thinking as they touch upon our existence in time and space. At times, they may be termed significant, and last as if in a glimpse or have a duration of many seconds depending on the moment's dual presence (Ansdell et al., 2010; Trondalen, 2005). The perception of the lived experience in the here and now is experienced at a subjective level connected to the living body. As one child said participating in a mother-child music group after eight hours in the kindergarten, 'I am not tired when we are singing like *this*' (Trolldalen, 1997, p. 14). Trusting each other, laying oneself open (Løgstrup, 1956/1997), through musicking led to situated appreciative recognition, independent of age and professional musical skills.

Time and space seem to be evident, for example, in a music listening procedure like Guided Imagery and Music (GIM), which includes listening to music in a relaxed state of mind. Allowing oneself to dwell in the music may affirm and constitute the potential power of music, for example, to professional musicians. One musician said when listening to music, 'I am receiving the music—just enjoying the music—I am changing through the music—I am open to the music now'. Another said, '[listening like] this is "nutrition" for the time to come' (Trondalen, 2016b, pp. 12–13). We might wonder if such opening and nurturing through music in time and space is in line with Higgins' displaying, '[Music] gives the listener a prereflective sense of *being* a self. Music gives us a sense of fully "being there" with our faculties fully engaged' (Higgins, 2011, p. 120). The music then supports our lives as temporal beings in time and space—with ethical dimensions of a 'good life'.

Allowing meaning to emerge and create in time and space gives associations to DeNora's (2014) methodological approach, 'slow sociology', an anti-generic mode of inquiry of investigating things in their particularity. The meaning-making process is based on particularities situated at a local level. Dwelling in music listening or active music making in time and space while paying attention to particularities at the local level is essential. Our ability to slow down and be present and aware influences our perception and capacity to control our lives. It affects the musical experience itself.

Such an influence of presence is also Johansson's point when she argues that listening to and expressing ourselves through music allows for in-depth awareness, presented through her focus on repetition and 'slow music therapy' (Johansson, 2017). Continuously unfolding moments, openness, movement, and difference are essential dimensions of being together in time. Such a musical lingering may create a space for valuing and enrichening the musical experience as a means of being per se, hence a 'good life'.

Also, the psychoanalyst Winnicott (1961, in Davis & Wallbridge, 2011, p. 169) is occupied with time and space, saying, 'Every life and every therapy session has its boundaries, provided by time'. Time is the 'the fourth dimension in integration'. As creative beings, we are offered a 'potential space' (Winnicott, 1971) for play, which takes place in between fantasy and reality. Such a potential space is necessary when painful incidents threaten our way of being. As human beings, we exist in a procedural continuum of time.

Nevertheless, we will always experience disruption in the perception of time, for example, when traumatic events impose on our usual way of living. Continuity fails; negative disruption is a fact (Knudsen et al., 2014). A breakdown in continuity most often influences one's capacity to unite the past with the present. Therefore, it might be hard to imagine the influences of the present upon the future. Musical engagement may potentially afford a way of restoring continuity; music presents as a lifeline, a holding and contained space, offering new ways of relating and connecting in time and space. Structure and continuity are organizing elements within a musically attuned relationship, enhancing renewed self-agency and continuity in the aftermath of traumatic experiences (Johns, 2008).

Musical engagement offers a potentially expanding experience, an interim in time and space—with ethical connotations. From a sociological point of view, such a musical time and potential space seem to be in line with DeNora's 'music asylum' (2013, p. 1), that is, 'a place and time in which it is possible to flourish'. Flourishing connects to the good life where play, rest, and creativity unfold through and in musicking. Here elucidated by one professional musician's commenting during music listening, 'New rooms are opening—I'm using my creativity in a new way—I'm experiencing the music in other ways than I've done before' (Trondalen, 2016b, p. 13). Such potentiality in time and space links to ethics through valuing music, enriching and manifesting positive values of a 'good life'.

## *Context and involvement*

In an ethical musicality, context and involvement refer to participatory engagement when dealing with philosophical, theoretical, and practical issues in an ethical endeavour. According to the Ancient Greek's 'doctrine of ethos', music had a formative moral power: music supported harmonic personalities and had a role in people's upbringing (D'Angour, 2021). In the 21st century, the post-modern or late area of modernity, the view upon music, musical development, and its function cover multiple spectres of understandings.

How music and ethics align changes due to different discourses, individual and social contexts, and the type and degree of involvement at different levels (Ruud, 2016). One aspect connects to the multiplicity of musical meanings and interpretations. Has music still some 'intrinsic power' even when interpreted from a constructivist point of view? What kinds of ethics elucidate the different genre and music experiences? (Higgins, 2011). Musical development and the necessary recognition of all types of music are tied to music's influence on our lives (Bartleet & Higgins, 2018).

Ethical musicality comes with a calling: self-critique as well as social critique, not least when researching music. Stige et al. (2009, p. 1510) draw attention to critical theory, feminism, and post-colonialist theory, focusing on power and privilege problems when evaluating (qualitative) research. They argue, 'These traditions are based on the assumption that all research is situated in social and political contexts'. Such a critical position assigns to all music professional in social and political considerations.

Furthermore, ethical musicality embraces music within various social contexts, with influences at a practical level. Ethical musicality commits to debating how philosophical and theoretical traditions situate reality through language and constituting actions in a musical setting. One example is the biomedical concept of health, which leads to a 'constant need of "repairing" and bridging the gap between bios and zoe, nature and culture' (Kristeva et al., 2018, p. 55). An alternative to such an instrumental way of thinking is a call for a radical medical humanity where culture acquires its natural place. Such a radical concern with cultural dimensions of health embraces body as a complex biocultural fact. In plain words, advocating culture as a healing factor may eventually lead to a rethinking of the concept of 'evidence' in healthcare. Thus, the influence of music has ethical implications for isolation, autonomy, and subjective involvement.

Ethical musicality also embraces *diversity* as an opening perspective to philosophy, intertextuality, research methods, and the practice of a wholesome life. Such a formative vision is deeply rooted in respect for the other. There are dark shadows in our music society related to race, gender spectrum, colour, ethnicity, age, religion, (dis)ableism, geographical region, neurodiversity, vocal opinion, social class, justice, (qualified)rights, cultural competence, power (im)balance, privilege, colonialism, and (un)equality. Each embedded content of the words above contains narratives of oppression and cultural biases. Sadly, there are too many references elucidating the previous sentence to include in this brief comment. When these shadows are seized, it is impossible to be indifferent!

In an interview on 'Affirmative ethics, posthuman subjectivity, and intimate scholarship', Braidotti argues,

> You can take any mechanism of capture whether it be race, ability, age, class they are mechanisms that shape bodies and experiences and force them into identity categories. In that respect, although identity is a necessary grammar of social interaction, it is also something that we need to move beyond. So, when we say nomadic politics is post-identitarian, this is not a way of despising or dismissing identity, but of exposing the power mechanisms that structure it. It is just a way of moving beyond what is ultimately a reactive formation.
>
> (Braidotti, 2018, p. 182)

Music is used in society and by individuals, music contributes to identity formation (MacDonald et al., 2017). Leaning towards an ethical musicality with diversity as an opening perspective, empowering people through musical involvement, is not only a task imposed upon us from an outside perspective. It is also an individual claim and endeavour when encountering others in their individuality or society. Such ethical beneficence is in line with Lévenesian philosophy: the face of the Other is the source of ethics (Lévinas, 1989). Therefore, no one can remain indifferent, untouched, or unresponsive, involved in an ethical musicality.

Asking questions and talking to each other allows for a reflecting way of dealing with ethical musicality. We learn from the Socratic method of dialogue, even if today's connotations and ethically loaded music understanding may differ from the Ancient Greeks'. In line with loaded connotations we ask, *can music be unethical*? According to Higgins (2011, p. 154), there are seven common arguments offered against music (or some kind of music) on ethical grounds. They are:

1. Music arouses passions that are harmful or difficult to control.
2. Music encourages the abandonment of reason.
3. Music lowers moral inhibitions.
4. Music excites sexual appetite.
5. Music glamorizes unethical causes.
6. Music encourages emotional support for questionable status quo.
7. Music distracts from more important concerns.

Higgins divides these arguments into two categories, which she labels in line with Nietzsche's terms *Dionysian* and *Apollonian*. The first four arguments link (some) music to a Dionysian way of living, inviting chaos and disruption, especially when it comes to erotic life. The latter three arguments belong to an Apollonian dispute. They augment that 'music fills our conscious minds or encourages our assent to inappropriate ideas' (p. 154)

The idea that some music is unethical needs to be debated and linked to context and involvement. By including knowledge from communicative musicality as a human capacity, (Malloch & Trevarthen, 2009a), neuroscience and brain research (Fachner et al., 2019; Wittmann, 2017), performance studies (Gillebo, 2018), and cultural studies in a broad sense (Bartleet & Higgins, 2018; DeNora, 2014; Dyndahl et al., 2020; McClary, 2002), we might open our minds to and beyond the question of potentially good or bad music, from ethical or unethical music, towards enjoying music as a suitable resource to enhance our ability to thrive.

An ethical musicality pays attention to prejudices and pre-decided meanings and values following our ethical considerations of music. We need to reflect through engagement, while processing and interpreting, touching on music and utility. Let us ask who, what, where, when, how, and why not? Continuously stressing the cognitive loaded 'why' may lead us away from music as an art form. Allowing music to be precisely what it is, an aesthetic art form in society, will enable us to question a possible dominance of narrow utilitarian thinking, which shows us music's vital usefulness (Varkøy, 2012).

Ethical musicality also involves individual and social choices linked to ways of living. Human beings are relational and potential contributors to a 'good life' through collaborative actions. In such a responsible human approach, values and a 'good life' are not solely linked to the music as an object as it also concerns how we situate ourselves and others in the world. Contextual involvement deals with no less than isolation, lack of community and privileged positions, that is, ecology in a broad sense. As relational beings, we are vulnerable *and* able to act, not least when working collaboratively. The latter may be illustrated by the people's involvement using music to protest, process, and (at some level) unite Norway after the terror attack on innocent young people on a political summer camp in 2011 (Skånland & Trondalen, 2014). Involving in collaborative singing, for example, seemed to promote connectedness and belonging, eventually, promoting sustainability. Ruud (2020, p. 127) argues,

> [a]n act of collaborative musicking may have implication for the arousal of shared intentionality, which again may be at the root of collective intentionality, where we as a group can handle social and political challenges.

Involvement and context matter. We link to each other through the multicultural dimension of networks of technologies, ideas, and social schemes.

These cultural intersections are observable through the various forms of musicking (DeNora, 2000; Ruud, 2020). Engaging in culturally and ethically informed music dialogues might counteract discrimination, oppression, and biases (Whitehead-Pleaux & Tan, 2016). Accordingly, responding to the strong tendencies towards individualism that characterizes many of today's music cultural attitudes.

## *Power and responsibility*

The following explores power and responsibility in an ethical musicality. Listening to music influences body and mind while offering value-based associations, symbols, and images. Expressing and listening to music are relational activities where the music and the context influence the experience. An ethical component in music links to a relational awareness offering recognition through music or the mutual appreciation in a joint musicking. The strong relationship between music and the musical relating experience arrives as opportunity and responsibility, of which we cannot be untouched (Løgstrup, 1956/1997).

Terms like right and wrong, good and evil, just and unfair are familiar to us (Farrant et al., 2014). However, *living ethics* is not the same as knowing about our values, rules, and regulations and their overlap with the law. 'Do no harm' (nonmaleficence) no longer seems to be enough to protect human dignity in an increasingly more complex society. One example is the principle of telling the truth (veracity). However, the truth is manifold in many cases and includes dilemmas with no fixed solution. Also, with all its opportunities and potential of harming, the digital age influences an ethical musicality as it intrinsically links to ecological and economic power. Accordingly, ethical assessments happen quickly and unpredictably, demanding an improvisational contextual involvement rooted in legal and ethics awareness. Ansdell says (2014a, p. 12),

> [a] postmodern view of ethics suggests that without firm, traditional religious or imposed political foundations, we need to improvise them ourselves, through dialogue and dispute about our values, and in response to those ever-fluid situation where we are challenged personally and communally by an ethical demand that we must approve of and act towards.

Therefore, 'do no harm' demands a situated awareness informed by the best legislation, recommendations, guidelines, and lived ethics available. Yet, 'do no harm' provides a steering compass for music professionals at different levels in various contexts, while upgrading freedom, vulnerability, dignity, and mercy as essentials for an ethical life (Nussbaum, 2011, 2021).

To exemplify these values, let us explore the musical listening mode Guided Imagery and Music, performed as a part of a personal developmental pursuit (Trondalen, 2009–2010, 2019b). There is an urgent need for an ethical sensitivity concerning anti-oppressive strategies and contextual situatedness embracing the music listener's vulnerability *and* autonomy in such a music listening procedure. Also, as the guide most often chooses the music on her/his own or in collaboration with the music listener, supervision is paramount. Supervision may include, for example, an exploration of a potential musical gendering of the instruments in the music chosen by the guide, as the musical instrumentation influences the experience (Hallsted & Rolvsjord, 2015). There is a need for extensive awareness at various levels of Guided Imagery and Music to counteract potential harm (nonmaleficence) and benefit the listener in her/his wholeness (Montgomery, 2019).

Aspects of power and responsibility may also be at stake within transcendent and spiritual experiences in daily music listening. For many people, music is linked with spiritual experiences and belong to the person's intimate, holy, and private space (Gabrielson, 2011; Pethybridge, 2013; Tsiris, 2017). Human spirituality connects to a universal phenomenon, which may involve longings for something life-giving, vitalizing, unifying, and integrative in life. Transcendent and spiritual music experiences go beyond the limited or controlled self and may touch the human's most profound value as a creation (Abrams, 2019).

Sometimes spiritual experiences through music do *not* lead to liberation, for example, when repression or imposed exposure of these practices is inspired by control, power, or simply by immaturity. Spiritual experiences through music may influence and change people, (religious) practices, and society. They may consciously or unconsciously threaten those in power to the degree that some call these musical experiences demonic. The theologian Laugerud (2012) argues that such a negatively oriented power may reduce life quality profoundly and serve to split and confuse. The influence of negative spiritual power may lessen by making these spiritual power structures transparent.

Furthermore, music may support destructive actions, which was the case when the white terrorist alone was responsible for bombing the government quarters and killing and injuring youngsters at a summer camp in Norway in 2011. According to his manifest, the terrorist used music to strengthen his power in 'actions of martyrdom' (Bjorøy & Hawkins, 2014, p. 139). The musicologists Bjorøy and Hawkins critically examine links between music, terror, and gender before they contemplate, 'And. Lest we forget, popular music was a principle constituent in the composite of this patriotic vehemence' (p. 158).

Another example where music is used for potential damage is the dark web, where self-esteem and life are in jeopardy. Dangerous liaisons between minors promote music for self-harm and destructive behaviour. Behind the shiny image on social media, there is an ongoing competition on living the most dreadful life. Dreadfulness is supported and valued through affirmative 'likes' (Moland, 2021). Hence, self-agency for the music listener is not a quality per se but something that arises within its situatedness.

Language and storytelling create narratives of musical realities (Bonde et al., 2013; Hadley, 2013; Norris, 2020). The social construction of language creates realities. However, whose realities in which time? What happens, for example, to the historical realities when documents worthy of preservation are deleted due to privacy? In line with the GDPR, researchers may be denied access to information about the individual's war crimes (Brottveidt, 2018). Accordingly, neither researchers nor the public will acquire information about if—and eventually when and where—music might have been misused during war crimes by individuals and authorities.

Music also creates realities. One example is the Norwegian record company's value-based response to the former President of the United States coining the 'axis of evil'. The record company *Kirkelig Kulturverksted* invited mothers from the regions along the axis to sing their local lullabies. The producer mixed the original voices of the mothers with Western female voices—*alongside* and *together*—in a musical web and named the album 'Lullabies from the axis of evil' (Various artists, 2004).

Another example of power and responsibility comes with research methodology and public presentations. For example, participants' voices grow as contributors to research themes and as co-researchers. Adding user's participation to the design can strengthen the study's validity and be seen as a user's right (Slotfeldt-Ellingsen, 2020). In some funding organizations, user participation is a prerequisite for economic funding and the implementation of a research study. Furthermore, laypeople engaged as researchers ('citizen science'; ECSA, 2015) can richly contribute to the study with, for example, cultural knowledge of local music. However, persons or groups with *one* privileged status of music taste might influence funders and authorities on what research is essential, negatively impacting various research opportunities over time. Another challenging aspect might be powerful user groups with *specific* agendas, for example, organizations with political or economic interests anticipating specific research results (Fugelsnes, 2019). Dilemmas increase when children and minors are involved.

What consequences do participation in a research project on music performance have in the long run? How does it feel observing oneself as very sick with Anorexia Nervosa in a video excerpt in an online conference presentation eight years after healing from the eating disorder? And not knowing the spread of the video clip due to the non-faced conference delegates or concert spectators participating from her/his dining room? Stigmatized? Empowered? It is reasonable that conferences and concert organizers increasingly include ethical guidelines in their call for papers and concert advertisements.

When research ethics is put under pressure, we should also discuss whether we should *reconsider* research ethics frameworks in a time of crisis or whether this is precisely the time when it is essential to *maintain* basic research ethics principles (Ingierd et al., 2021). Hence, the item of ethics itself must always be a subject of inspection to promote a detailed and disciplined *lived ethics* through integrity personally, professionally, and socially.

An ethical musicality invites balancing power and responsibility. It is a calling to raise awareness of non-judging and explorative involvement through philosophical endeavour, research, and responsible practices to shed light upon pre-judges and negative *and* life-giving influences of music. Such a responsible awareness addresses personal and social trust linked to national and international diversities in power and responsibility, involving a continuous, systematic reflection to develop as broad and dynamic ethical competence as possible under ever-changing conditions.

## *Sustainability and hope*

The last pairing of words towards an ethical musicality is sustainability and hope. Sustainability often presents three pillars—economic and environmental endeavours, in addition to social emphasis. As human beings, we develop through relationships with people *and* contexts. We commit to the UN Sustainable Developmental Goals, Agenda 2030 (UN, 2015) from this existential position. As a part of an ecological system, such ethical perseverance exemplifies through the value-based concepts of *capability*, *health*, and the *paradox of freedom*, illustrating music as a vital ethical component contributing to sustainability and hope.

*Capabilities* connect with the 'Capability Approach' (Nussbaum, 2011). The theory of analysing the human condition coins the individual dignity, vulnerability, and actual freedom, namely, her/his capability to choose between what can be done (realized) and the freedom and values from which one can choose (effectively possible) (Nussbaum, 2011; Robeyns, 2013). Embedded in Nussbaum's thinking is a concern with the capabilities of nonhuman animals as well as human beings (2011, p. 18).

But what are *capabilities*? Nussbaum says, 'They are the answers to the question, "What is this person able to do and to be?"' She replies with reference to what Sen (1985/1999) calls 'substantial freedoms', a set of (usually interrelated) opportunities to choose and to act (in Nussbaum, 2011, p. 20). In Nussbaum's words,

> they are not just abilities residing inside a person but also the freedoms or opportunities created by a combination of personal abilities and the political, social, and economic environment.
>
> (p. 20)

Nussbaum refers to these 'substantial freedoms' as *combined capabilities* while adding, the notion *internal capabilities*.

> [Internal capabilities] are to be distinguished from innate equipment: they are trained or developed traits and abilities, developed, in most cases, in interaction with the social, economic, familial, and political environment.
>
> (p. 21)

Internal capabilities relate to skills that transfer to the musical scene, such as playing the drum kit or gaining self-confidence through musicking. To accentuate, internal capabilities in a Capability Approach are *not* equivalent to an innate psycho-biological capacity, such as communicative musicality (Malloch & Trevarthen, 2009b). Internal capabilities are skills cultivated in context.

However, a move *towards* internal capabilities may develop on the basis of the caregivers bringing components from their musical culture into the proto- and turn-taking communication, for example, lullabies (Bonnár, 2014) and nursery rhymes. These expressions with cultural bearings will eventually affect the dyadic procedural communication at a local level, leading to a 'we' *in* culture (Pavlicevic & Andsdell, 2009, p. 364). That said, it is not only the accumulation of the dyadic musical communication between a caregiver and the infant but the 'facilitation of paradyadic musical experiences' that makes collaborative musicing (sic.) possible (pp. 364–365). Inborn capacities *are* different from internal capabilities. But we may speculate as it might seem unlikely that internal capabilities are created without an inborn capacity for communication through musical dynamics.

Creating capabilities is vital. There is, however, a tension between internal and combined capabilities: a girl may have acquired skills to play the viola at school (internally capable). She takes great joy in playing and longs for playing in the local children's symphony orchestra as a leisure activity. But due to her family's negative attitude toward such a cultural activity per se, or because her family has a disadvantaged economic position (combined capability)—an opportunity to function in accordance with her capabilities is cut off.

In short, capabilities refer to real opportunities: 'both what we are able to do (activities), as well as the kind of person we can be (dimensions of our being)' called (human) *functionings* (Robeyns, 2013, p. 413). Nussbaum clarifies,

> [b]ecause combined capabilities are defined as internal capabilities plus the social/political/economic conditions in which functioning can actually be chose, it is not possible conceptually to think of a society producing combined capabilities without producing internal capabilities.
>
> (2011, p. 22)

Capabilities are a person's *real* freedom to choose or opportunities to achieve functioning. These functionings are not achieved in any way but in a genuinely human way, for example, self-expressive creativity. However, as we saw in the illustration with the child and her instrument, she had the functioning but was not able to choose where to play, that is, capability. Hence, people experience unequal capabilities due to economic, environmental, and social factors. A Capability Approach is, therefore, a matter of ethical concern.

Technology plays a role in an ethical musicality. When afforded and appropriated, technological advancements such as welfare technologies, telehealth, artificial intelligence, and new virtual reality approaches may support human capabilities. One example of such a humane welfare technology is the information and communication technologies (ICT)-based 'co-creative tangibles', aiming at reducing isolation and passivity for families with children with severe disabilities. The technology builds upon computer-based interactive sound design, exploring vocal, bodily, and tactile interaction as *input*—and music, tactile sensations, and lighting as *output*. These co-creative 'things' are collaborative, tangible, interactive Internet-based musical 'smart things' with multimedia capabilities. They can be moved around, are networked and multimodal, and communicate following musical, narrative, and communicative principles (Andersson & Cappelen, 2014). Through their interactive, social, and intelligent 'co-creative tangibles' affordances, they have proved to motivate play, communication and co-creation, reduce passivity and isolation, strengthen health and well-being (Stensæth, 2018), hence, contributing to optimism and hope.

Music affects our moods, emotions, and ways of living today (MacDonald et al., 2012), as throughout history (Horden, 2000). Music may offer cultural meaning, values, hope, and a sense of agency; function as a 'cultural immunogen' (Ruud, 2020, p. 48), and be associated with social determinants of well-being and good health. Such action and performance-based 'health musicking' (Stige, 2018) connects to capabilities in terms of what music offers and ways of using those potentials (Ansdell, 2014b).

Music may also address health needs in a concrete way. Within areas with low levels of literacy and limited access to electronic media, live music and performance may be used to communicate public health messages, straightforwardly or more implicitly. 'Such interventions often reference local music-making traditions and thus have a strong potential for local sustainability' (Howell, 2018, p. 51). Paradoxically, these musical involvements may also positively impact the health messengers themselves, hence promoting sustainability at a personal level.

Different factors affect the sustainability of music professionals, personally and professionally. To prevent stress and burnout, music professionals need to address self-care, and a work-life balance, in order to promote 'a good life', that is, an ethical life. Such an exploration may include biology (i.e. physical elements), psychological issues (mental state, existential being), and context (work setting and home/social context) while also keeping in mind the freedom of playing or listening to music as a source of inspiration in itself. Music is essential to music professionals in their professional jobs and indeed linked to their core (Trondalen, 2016c).

Sustainability is indeed a mulitlayered phenomena. The same can be said about freedom, as with *freedom* comes opportunities and, eventually, choices. These choices are potentially present as *paradoxes*. One enlightening example is presented in the article 'Professional reflexivity and the paradox of freedom: Negotiating professional boundaries in a Jewish Ultra-Orthodox female music teacher education programme' (Westerlund et al., 2021). The researchers interviewed and generated data together with six all-female music teacher educators. Results showed that the teachers accommodated the music programmes within religious boundaries. When the music genre presented a societal and value-based challenge due to its content, the teachers applied context-sensitive approaches negotiating their professional and value-based boundaries by such as keeping the music but changing the lyrics or including prayer songs in the music repertoire. The music teacher educators continuously performed reflexivity on their choices 'to ensure that their professional choices were always in service of their society and their values' (p. 432). The results convey to all involved in music education, encouraging a critical inspection of how ethically driven values are present in, for example, the hidden curriculum (Baines et al., 2019; Johansen, 2021).

Music in peace and conflict resolution is another area shedding light upon the paradox of freedom. For example, the Russian cellist Mstislav Rostropóvich chose to perform music as an encouraging response to people destroying the Berlin Wall in Germany (11 November 1989), while Bruce Springsteen wrote 'The Wall' in 1997 after visiting the Vietnam Veterans Memorial in Washington. Music links closely to important socio-political movements. The song 'We shall overcome' is a signifying music statement of the Civil Rights Movement for equal rights for African-Americans in the 1950s and 1960s. Similarly, 'Venceremos' ('We shall overcome') was used as a means of political expression (Higgins, 2008) during the struggle for freedom from the Chilean dictatorship in 1973.

South Africa chose to include communal singing of hymns along with the national anthem every session during the work of their Truth and Reconciliation Commission's task to promote a transition to majority rules in the 1990s (Philips-Hutton, 2020). Also, Ukrainian women, children, and youngsters sing while making bandages or camouflage tents from torn strips of fabric in gymnasiums and assembly halls. The songs are about daily life—and the national anthem often sounds.

Furthermore, Indigenous music sustainability is put under pressure. Today's news reminds us of how the Sámi, the Indigenous people of Norway, were sentenced to death on a bonfire only a century ago due to their shamanistic use of drums—while still experiencing musical discrimination (Skartland & Ebeltoft, 2022, 11 February). Indigenous music sustainability is challenged due to, for example, climate change and forced geographical and cultural assimilation and replacement. Also, Indigenous music often links to cultures, places, and the natural landscape. Climate change and, eventually, ecosystems threaten the musical culture, and the availability of natural materials for musical instruments is also in jeopardy (Harrison, 2019).

Peace, conflict, terror, trauma, and potential reconciliation have indeed many faces. In her text *Music transforming conflicts*, Ariana Philips-Hutton (2020) draws attention to the moral shadows performed by the assumption of white supremacy in society. She says, 'knowledge is a necessary but not sufficient condition for transformative change' (p. 60). We say: an ethical musicality is not only timely but necessary.

We need to enhance music strategies to advance humanization, creating hope. But how? Music as an embodied experience has the potential of transcending 'barriers and forge some sense of solidarity even among people who consider themselves to be enemies'. Higgins refers to the tale of combatants putting away their weapons at Christmas during World War I in December 1914, where songs might have eased the tension embedded in anxiety and fear. She suggests that music 'offers an education in living humanely' (Higgins, 2008, pp. 389–390). Also, in post-conflict contexts, musicking may offer a normality in a challenged everyday life. Instrument learning, band playing, performance, studio work, and accompanying other art-based approaches are musical affordances, a 'cultural aid' in a post-conflict recovery (Howell, 2018).

Likewise, some music and lyrics seem to grasp our full capabilities and offer existential meaning. At other times, we need another to carry our hope: 'I had no hope then you were my hope and when I got healthier, I managed to hope for myself' (Hagen, 2020, p. 39). Time is hope. As a creative act, music offers a unique opportunity to be renewed in the present, a renewed identity 'infected' by hope (Aldridge, 1999).

Active participation and dialoguing through critical negotiation are ontological necessities for promoting humanistic values. Dialogue is hope (Freire, 1970). Hope may be more or less likely—but never unimportant. At times, music offers a breathing space in time, a creative way of dealing with life itself, affording hope.

> [H]ope is the ultimate dream we carry—when we hope we are imbued with purpose and meaning, and we are connected to a vision of the world . . . thereby making what is dreamed of as the future present.
>
> (DeNora, 2021, p. 128)

Music becomes a part of ethical living, in which we may insert our whole lifeworld. In such a life web, ethical musicality unites with sustainability and hope.

## Ethical musicality: an art of becoming

Music offers existential dimensions unlike anything else. When capturing the phenomenon in words, we leave the phenomenal music experience per se. Moving from the direct (immediate) experience while trying to explain through (mediated) language, the multidimensional embodied experience reduces and transforms. The fullness of music cannot be captured in words when it touches, emerges, creates, and performs in sociality—in the present moment. Music is something else and always more than—*Semper major*—what meets the eye.

An ethical musicality combines a music-philosophical discourse of music and ethics with musical ethics' practical crossroads. It unifies these elaborations with the four fundamental existentials of being in the world, body, relationship, time, and space, in addition to the lived phenomena of context, involvement, power, responsibility, sustainability, and hope. When tied together, music and ethics link profoundly. An ethical musicality emerges and creates in sociality within an ecological context—in the present moment—while pointing to a *lived* ethical musicality.

An ethical musicality offers a welcome to surrender and dwell in a musical presence. Such a presence heavily depends on the closeness between the two phenomena of music and ethics, as they—when tied together—offer real-life perspectives that would otherwise be inaccessible to us.

We appreciate the powerful influence of music on people's lives, ways of being and understanding, that is, affecting a 'good life'. Music does not leave us untouched; an ethical musicality represents an ongoing *calling*. A call to surrender (to the music), share, act, involve, do good, and care—to become musical humans recognising that music changes people's *real* lives.

From a philosophical point of view, responding to such a calling never reduces the Other to sameness (totality) (Lévinas, 1961/2012). On the contrary, we open ourselves to something radically different leading to maintaining the Other's integrity (infinity). The Face of the Other, *and 'The Third'* (Face–the Other–to us, Nortvedt, 1996), we argue, make us to something we cannot be on our own. The Face(s) becomes the carrier of an ethical demand (Løgstrup, 1956/1997).

In these Face(s), we meet each other with a vulnerability not open to negotiation, and therefore it is not possible to be indifferent and unresponsive. Ethical musicality involves values and trust, openness (embodied knowledge), relational engagement, mutual respect (uniqueness), and context sensitivity (i.e. creating environment) *within* an ecological system.

By being in the world, we are made ethically receptible and responsible to a world *in-becoming*. This response includes presence and care and an obligation of being for the Other (Thomassen, 2019). Such a being focuses dependency and vulnerability following always given to each other. However, an ethical musicality engagement is not only a Lévenesian 'passive undertaking'. On the contrary, an ethical and active musicality 'demands the responsible and responsive engagement of critical agents who commit themselves to explanation' (Cobussen & Nielsen, 2012/2016, p. 155). An ethical musicality is an invitation and a welcome to commit to such an art form of becoming—offering hope of a 'good life'.

## Summary

Having offered a music-philosophical discourse of music and ethics and musical ethics' practical crossroads, we turned to the reflexivity of music and ethics. First, we focused on the conceptual basis for ethical musicality, illustrating that ethical musically creates from prevailing and emergent ideas of knowing *in becoming*. We next explored the notion of musicality, unfolding through communicative musicality, musicianship, and culture, eventually suggesting musicality as an existential dimension of seizing, absorbing, and participating in various modes of embodied musical experiences, a *lived experience*.

Furthermore, an ethical musicality unfolds through the four fundamental existentials of being in the world—the body, relationship, time, and space. Following these existentials, the chapter expanded on context, involvement, power, responsibility, sustainability, and hope. Finally, when tying the music-ethical discourse and the musical ethics' practical crossroads to

Reflexivity 83

fundamental existentials and different cultures of ethical musicality involvement, an ethical musicality emerges and creates in sociality—in the present moment—with ethical implications.

Ethical musicality is a shaping of thoughts and ideas merged into a *conceptual framework*—with existential implications. The chapter illustrates an ethical musicality coming with a calling *to* humanity in a broad sense, which does not leave us untouched. Such a calling comprehends a call to surrender, share, act, involve, do good, and care—to become musical humans recognizing that music changes people's *real* lives. Hence, an ethical musicality is an invitation and a welcome to commit to such an art form of becoming—offering hope of a 'good life'.

## References

Abrams, B. (2019). Transpersonal dimensions of the Bonny method of Guided Imagery and Music (BMGIM). In D. Grocke (Ed.), *Guided imagery and music: The Bonny method and beyond* (2nd ed., pp. 383–397). Dallas, TX: Barcelona Publishers.

Aldridge, D. (1996). *Music therapy research and practice in medicine. From out of the silence.* London: Jessica Kingsley Publishers.

Aldridge, D. (1999). Music therapy and the creative act. In D. Aldridge (Ed.), *Music therapy in palliative care. New voices* (pp. 9–28). London and Philadelphia: Jessica Kingsley Publishers.

Andersson, A.-P., & Cappelen, B. (2014). Vocal and tangible interaction in RHYME. In K. Stensæth (Ed.), *Music, health, technology and design* (Vol. 8, NMH-Publications, pp. 21–38). Oslo: CREMAH, Norwegian Academy of Music.

Ansdell, G. (2014a). Foreword. 'Infinitely demanding': The creative work of research ethics. In C. Farrant, M. Pavlicevic, & G. Tsiris (Eds.), *A guide to research ethics for art therapists and arts and health practitioners* (pp. 11–15). London and Philadelphia: Jessica Kingsley Publishers.

Ansdell, G. (2014b). *How music helps in music therapy and everyday life.* Ashgate: Farnham.

Ansdell, G., Davidson, J., Magee, W., Meehan, J., & Procter, S. (2010). From 'this ****ing life' to 'that's better' . . . . in four minutes: An interdisciplinary study of music therapy's 'present moments' and their potential for affect modulation. *Nordic Journal of Music Therapy, 19*(1), 3–28. http://doi.org/10.1080/08098130903407774.

Baines, S., Pereira, J., Hatch, J., & Edwards, J. (2019). Queering the curriculum: Why music therapy and other creative arts therapy trainings need queer theory. *Voices. A World Forum for Music Therapy, 19*(3). http://doi.org/10.15845/voices.v19i3.2676.

Bartleet, B.-L., & Higgins, L. (Eds.). (2018). *The Oxford handbook of community music.* Oxford and New York: Oxford University Press.

Bateson, M. C. (1975). Mother-infant exchanges: The epigenesis of conversational interaction. *New York Academy of Sciences. Annals* (263), 101–113.

Benestad, F. (1976). *Musikk og tanke. Hovedretninger i musikkestetikkens historie fra antikken til vår egen tid (Music and thought. Main directions in the history of music aesthetics from Antiquity to our time)*. Oslo: Aschehoug.

Bjorøy, K.-M., & Hawkins, S. (2014). "When light turn into darkness". Inscriptions of music and terror in Oslo 22 July 2011. In J. S. Knudsen, M. S. Skånland, & G. Trondalen (Eds.), *Musikk etter 22. juli (Music in the aftermath of 22 July)* (Vol. 5, NMH-Publications, pp. 139–162). Oslo: CREMAH, Norges musikkhøgskole.

Bonde, L. O., Ruud, E., Skånland, M. S., & Trondalen, G. (Eds.). (2013). *Musical life stories. Narratives on health musicking* (Vol. 5, NMH-Publications). Oslo: CREMAH, Norges musikkhøgskole.

Bonnár, L. (2014). *Life and lullabies. Exploring the basis of parents' lullaby singing* (PhD). Norwegian Academy of Music, Norway.

Bordieu, P. (1998). *Practical reason. On the theory of action*. Cambridge: Stanford University Press.

Braidotti, R. (2018). Affirmative ethics, posthuman subjectivity, and intimate scholarship: A conversation with Rosi Braidotti. In *Decentering the researcher in intimate scholarship: Critical posthuman methodological perspectives in education (Advances in research on teaching)* (Vol. 31, pp. 179–188). Bingley: Emerald Publishing Limited. https://doi.org/10.1108/S1479-368720180000031014.

Brottveidt, K. A. (2018). Personvern. Kritisk til GDPR. (Privacy. Critical of the GDPR). *Forskerforum. Tidsskrift for forskerforbundet, 7*.

Bruner, J. S. (1990). *Acts of meaning*. Cambridge: Harvard University Press.

Butler, J. (1993). *Bodies that matter*. New York and London: Routledge.

Christensen, E. (2012). *Music listening, music therapy, phenomenology and neuroscience* (PhD). Aalborg University, Denmark.

Cobussen, M., & Nielsen, N. (2012/2016). *Music and ethics*. London and New York: Routledge.

Cross, I., & Tolbert, E. (2021). Epistemologies. In T. Mcauley, N. Nielsen, J. Levinson, & A. Phillips-Hutton (Eds.), *The Oxford handbook of Western music and philosophy* (pp. 265–282) Oxford: Oxford University Press.

D'Angour, A. (2021). Ancient Greece. In T. McAuley, N. Nielsen, J. Levinson, & A. Phillips-Hutton (Eds.), *The Oxford handbook of Western music and philosophy* (pp. 117–135). Oxford: Oxford University Press.

Davis, M., & Wallbridge, D. (2011). *Boundary and space. An introduction to the work of D.W. Winnicott*. New York: Brunner-Routledge.

Deleuze, G., & Guattari, F. (1991/1994). *What is philosophy?* New York: Columbia University Press.

DeNora, T. (2000). *Music in everyday life*. Cambridge: Cambridge University Press.

DeNora, T. (2013). *Music asylums. Wellbeing through music in everyday life*. Farnham and Burlington: Ashgate.

DeNora, T. (2014). *Making sense of reality. Culture and perception in everyday life*. London: SAGE.

DeNora, T. (2021). *Hope. The dream we carry*. Cham, Switzerland: Palgrave Macmillan.

Dyndahl, P., Karlsen, S., & Wright, R. (Eds.). (2020). *Musical gentrification. Popular music, distinction and social mobility*. London: Routledge.

ECSA. (2015). *European citizen science association. Ten principles of citizen science*. Berlin. http://doi.org/10.17605/OSF.IO/XPR2N.

Elblaus, L., Hansen, K. F., & Unander-Sharin, C. (2012). Artistically directed prototyping in development in practice. *Journal of New Music Research, 41*(4), 377–387.

Fachner, J. C., Maidhof, C., Grocke, D., Pedersen, I. N., Trondalen, G., Tucek, G., & Bonde, L. O. (2019). "Telling me not to worry . . ." Hyperscanning and neural dynamics of emotion processing during guided imagery and music. *Frontiers in Psychology*. http://doi.org/10.3389/fpsyg.2019.01561.

Farrant, C., Pavlicevic, M., & Tsiris, G. (2014). *A guide to research ethics for arts therapists and arts and health practitioners*. London and Philadelphia: Jessica Kingsley Publishers.

Ferrara, L. (1991). *Philosophy and the analysis of music. Bridges to musical sound, form, and reference*. New York, Westport, CT and London: Greenwood Press.

Føllesdal, D. (1993). Edmund Husserl. In T. B. Eriksen (Ed.), *Vestens tenkere (Western thinkers)* (Vol. 3, pp. 168–188). Oslo: H. Aschehoug & Co. (W. Nygaard).

Freire, P. (1970). *Pedagogy of the oppressed*. New York: Continuum.

Fugelsnes, E. (2019). Vi må ikke la mektige brukere ta kontrollen (We must not let powerful users take control). *Forskningsetikk* (4), 16–17.

Gabrielson, A. (2011). *Strong experiences with music. Music is much more than just music*. Oxford: Oxford University Press.

Gillebo, M. (2018). *Singing reality. To sing as ethical demand and public discourse*. Paper presented at the Cultural Crossings of Care–An Appeal to the Medical Humanities, University of Oslo, October 26.

Hadley, S. (2013). *Experiencing race as a music therapist: Personal narratives*. Gilsum: Barcelona Publishers.

Hagen, M. (2020). *Håp i musikkterapi. En kvalitativ studie om hvilken rolle håp kan ha i musikkterapeuters arbeid innen psykisk helsevern* (Hope in music therapy. A qualitative study of the role of hope in music therapists' work in mental health care) (Masteroppgave i musikkterapi). Oslo: Norges musikkhøgskole.

Hallsted, J., & Rolvsjord, R. (2015). The gendering of musical instruments: What is that? Why does it matter to music therapy? *Nordic Journal of Music Therapy*. http://doi.org/10.1080/08098131.2015.1088057.

Harrison, K. (2019). Indigenous music sustainability during climate change. *Current Opinion in Environmental Sustainability, 43*, 28–34. doi:10.1016/j.cosust.2020.01.003.

Hatfield, J. L., & Lemyre, P.-N. (2016). Foundations of intervention research in instrumental practice: Constructing a psychological skills intervention for musicians. *Frontiers in Psychology*. http://doi.org/10.3389/psyg.2015.02014.

Higgins, K. M. (2008). Musical education for peace. In R. T. Ames & P. D. Hershock (Eds.), *Educations and their purposes* (pp. 389–404). Honolulu: University of Hawaii Press.

Higgins, K. M. (2011). *The music of our lives*. Lanham, Boulder, New York, Toronto and Plymouth, UK: Lexington Books.

Holgersen, S.-E. (2006). Den kropslige vending. En fænomenologisk undersøgelse af musikalsk intersubjektivitet. (The bodily turn. A phenomenological investigation

of musical intersubjectivity). In F. V. Nielsen & S. G. Nielsen (Eds.), *Nordisk musikkpedagogisk årbok* (Vol. 8, pp. 33–57). Oslo: Norges musikkhøgskole.
Horden, P. (Ed.). (2000). *Music as medicine. The history of music therapy since Antiquity*. Aldershot, Burlington USA, Singapore and Sidney: Ashgate.
Howell, G. (2018). Community music interventions in post-conflict contexts. In B.-L. Bartleet & L. Higgins (Eds.), *The Oxford handbook of community music* (pp. 43–70). Oxford and New York: Oxford University Press.
Ingierd, H., Iversen, C. B., & Bakstad, B. (2021). Når etikken settes på prøve (When ethics is put to the test). *Morgenbladet*, February 14. Retrieved from www.mor genbladet.no/ideer/kronikk/2021/02/14/nar-etikken-settes-pa-prove/.
Jegerstedt, K. (2008). Judith Butler. In E. Mortensen, C. Egeland, R. Gressgård, C. Holst, K. Jegerstedt, S. Rosland, & K. Sampson (Eds.), *Kjønnsteori (Gender theory)* (pp. 74–86). Oslo: Gyldendal akademisk.
Johansen, G. (2021). The hidden curriculum in higher music education. In R. Wright, G. Johansen, P. A. Kanellopoulos, & P. Schmidt (Eds.), *The Routledge handbook to sociology of music education*. London: Routledge.
Johansson, K. (2017). *Gjentakelse i musikkterapi (Repetition in music therapy)* (PhD). Norwegian Academy of Music, Norway.
Johns, U. T. (2008). "Å bruke tiden—hva betyr det egentlig". Tid og relasjon-et intersubjektivt perspektiv. ("Using the time—what does it really mean?" Time and relation—an intersubjective perspective). In G. Trondalen & E. Ruud (Eds.), *Perspektiver på musikk og helse (Perspectives on music and health)* (Vol. 8, NMH-publikasjoner, pp. 67–84). Oslo: CREMAH, Norges Musikkhøgskole.
Johns, U. T. (2018). Exploring musical dynamics in therapeutic interplay with children: A multi-layered method of microanalysis. *Nordic Journal of Music Therapy*, *27*(3). http://doi.org/10.1080/08098131.2017.1421685.
Jørgensen, H., & Lehmann, A. C. (Eds.). (1997). *Does practice make perfect? Current theory and research on instrumental music practice*, (NMH-publikasjoner, Vol. 1). Oslo: Norges musikkhøgskole.
Kallevik, S. A. (2007). Øyeblikkets betydning i mesterlig mestermøte (The importance of the moment in masterful meeting of masters). *Tidsskrift for Norsk Psykologforening*, *44*(10), 1261–1263.
Knudsen, J. S., Skånland, M. S., & Trondalen, G. (Eds.). (2014). *Musikk etter 22. juli (Music in the aftermath of 22 July)* (NMH-publikasjoner, Vol. 5). Oslo: CREMAH, Norges musikkhøgskole.
Kristeva, J., Moro, M. R., Ødemark, J., & Engebretsen, E. (2018). Cultural crossings of care: An appeal to the medical humanities. *Medical Humanities*, *44*, 55–58. doi:10.1136/medhum-2017-011263.
Langer, S. K. (1942/1974). *Philosophy in a new key. A study of symbolism of reason, rite, and art* (3rd ed.). Cambridge, MA: Harvard University Press.
Langer, S. K. (1953/1973). *Feeling and form. A theory of art developed from philosophy in a new key*. London: Routledge and Kegan Paul Limited.
Laugerud, T. (2012). Kirken i møte med åndelige erfaringer i grenselandet til kristen tro-et missiologisk perspektiv. (The church encountering spiritual experiences in the borderlands of Christian faith—a missiological perspective). *Tidsskrift for Praktisk Teologi*, *29*(1), 4–12.

Lévinas, E. (1961/2012). *Totality and infinity. An essay on exteriority* (A. Lingis, Trans.). Pittsburgh: Duquesne University Press.
Lévinas, E. (1989). Ethics as first philosophy. In S. Hand (Ed.), *The Levinas reader* (pp. 75–87). Oxford: Blackwell.
Løgstrup, K. E. (1956/1997). *The ethical demand* (T. I. Jensen, G. Puckering, & E. Watkins, Trans.). Notre Dame and London: University of Notre Dame Press.
MacDonald, R., Hargreaves, D. J., & Miell, D. (Eds.). (2017). *Handbook of musical identities*. Oxford: Oxford University Press.
MacDonald, R., Kreutz, G., & Mitchell, L. (2012). *Music, health, wellbeing*. Oxford: Oxford University Press.
Malloch, S., & Trevarthen, C. (2009a). *Communicative musicality. Exploring the basis of human companionship*. Oxford: Oxford University Press.
Malloch, S., & Trevarthen, C. (2009b). Musicality: Communicating the vitality and interests of life. In S. Malloch & C. Trevarthen (Eds.), *Communicative musicality. Exploring the basis of human companionship* (pp. 1–11). Oxford: Oxford University Press.
McClary, S. K. (2002). *Feminist endings: Music, gender, and sexuality* (2nd ed.). Minneapolis: University of Minnesota Press.
Merleau-Ponty, M. (1945/89). *Phenomenology and perception*. London: Routledge.
Moland, A. (2021). *Det skjulte nettverket. Farlige forbindler mellom unge på nettet. (The hidden network. Dangerous connections between young people online)*. Oslo: Cappelen Damm.
Montgomery, E. (2019). Ethical practice of Guided Imagery and Music. In D. E. Grocke (Ed.), *Guided imagery and music: The Bonny method and beyond* (2nd ed., pp. 675–687). Dallas, TX: Barcelona Publishers.
Nielsen, S. G., Johansen, G. G., & Jørgensen, H. (2018). Peer learning in instrumental practicing. *Frontiers in Psychology*, 9. http://doi.org/10.3389/fpsyg.2018.00339.
Norris, M. S. (2020). Freedom dreams: What must die in music therapy to preserve human dignity? *Voices: A World Forum for Music Therapy*, *20*(3). http://doi.org/10.15845/voices.v20i3.3172.
Nortvedt, P. (1996). Veien over til Den tredje (The road over to the Third). In A. J. Vetlesen (Ed.), *Nærhetsetikk (Ethics of care)* (pp. 139–158). Oslo: Ad Notam Gyldendal.
Nussbaum, M. C. (2011). *Creating capabilities. The human development approach*. Cambridge, MA: The Belknap Press of Harvard University Press.
Nussbaum, M. C. (2021). Mercy. In T. T. Mcauley, N. Nielsen, J. Levinson, & A. Phillips-Hutton (Eds.), *The Oxford handbook of Western music and philosophy* (pp. 803–822). Oxford: Oxford University Press.
Papousêk, M., & Papousêk, H. (1981). Musical elements in the infant's vocalization: Their significance for communication, cognition and creativity. In L. P. Lipsitt (Ed.), *Advances in infancy research* (Vol. 1, pp. 163–224). Norwood, NJ: Ablex.
Pavlicevic, M., & Andsdell, G. (2009). Between communicative musicality and collaborative musicing. In S. Malloch & C. Trevarthen (Eds.), *Communicative musicality. Exploring the basis of human companionship* (pp. 357–376). Oxford: Oxford University Press.
Pethybridge, E. (2013). Inner spirit: Investigating how music therapists' experiences of their spirituality may be relevant to their work. *British Journal of Music Therapy*, *27*, 40–51.

Philips-Hutton, A. (2020). Music transforming conflicts. In M. Cooke (Ed.), *Elements in music since 1945*. Cambridge: Cambridge Elements, Cambridge University Press.

Phillips-Hutton, A., & Nielsen, N. (2021). Ethics. In T. Mcauley, N. Nielsen, J. Levinson, & A. Phillips-Hutton (Eds.), *The Oxford handbook of Western music and philosophy* (pp. 283–306). Oxford: Oxford University Press.

Robeyns, I. (2013). Capability ethics. In H. Lafollette & I. Persson (Eds.), *The Blackwell guide to ethical theory* (2nd ed., pp. 412–432). West Sussex: Wiley Blackwell.

Ruud, E. (2016). *Musikkvitenskap (Musicology)*. Oslo: Universitetsforlaget.

Ruud, E. (2020). *Towards a sociology of music therapy: Musicking as a cultural immunogen*. Dallas, TX: Barcelona Publishers.

Sen, A. (1985/1999). *Commodities and capabilities*. Oxford: Oxford University Press.

Skartland, E., & Ebeltoft, L. B. (2022). Lone ble truet og spyttet etter: Det er et traume (Lone was threatened and spat on: It's a trauma). *Norwegian Broadcasting Cooperation (NRK)*. Retrieved from www.nrk.no/sapmi/lone-fra-vardo-ble-hetset-pa-grunn-av-trommen-1.15841554.

Skånland, M. S., & Trondalen, G. (2014). Music and grief: Norway After 22 July, 2011. *Voices: A World Forum for Music Therapy, 14*(2), 10. https://voices.no/index.php/voices/article/view/2230/1985.

Slotfeldt-Ellingsen, D. (2020). *Forskningsetikk. Yrkesetikk ved forskningsvirksomhet (Research ethics. Professional ethics in research)*. Oslo: Universitetsforlaget.

Stensæth, K. (Ed.). (2014). *Music, health, technology and design* (Vol. 8, NMH-Publications). Oslo: CREMAH, Norwegian Academy of Music.

Stensæth, K. (2018). Music as participation! Music as a novel means for health promoting participation with potentials to avoid isolation. In L. O. Bonde & T. Theorell (Eds.), *Music and public health: A Nordic perspective* (pp. 129–146). London: Springer Publishing Company.

Stern, D. N. (2000). *The Interpersonal world of the infant. A view from psychoanalysis & developmental psychology*. New York: Basic Books.

Stern, D. N. (2004). *The present moment in psychotherapy and everyday life*. New York and London: W. W. Norton & Company.

Stern, D. N. (2010). *Forms of vitality: Exploring dynamic experience in psychology, the arts, psychotherapy, and development*. Oxford and New York: Oxford University Press.

Stige, B. (2018). Partnership for health musicking: A case for connecting music therapy and public health practices. In L. O. Bonde & T. Theorell (Eds.), *Music and public health: A Nordic perspective*. Cham, CH: Springer.

Stige, B., Malterud, K., & Midtgarden, T. (2009). Toward an agenda for evaluation of qualitative research. *Qualitative Health Research, 19*(10), 1504–1516. doi:10.1177/1049732309348501.

Thomassen, M. (2019). Menneskets menneskelighet. Frihet og ansvar i Emmanuel Lévinas filosofi (Human humanity. Freedom and responsibility in Emmanuel Lévinas' philosophy). *SEGL—Katolsk Årsskrift for Religion og Samfunn*, 103–111.

Trevarthen, C. (1980). The foundations of intersubjectivity: Development of interpersonal and cooperative understanding in infants. In D. R. Olson (Ed.), *The social foundations of language and thought* (pp. 316–342). New York: Norton.

Trevarthen, C. (1999). Musicality and the intrinsic motive pulse: Evidence from human psychobiology and infant communication. *Musicæ Scientiæ. Escom European Society for the Cognitive Sciences of Music* (Special issue 1999–2000), 155–215.

Trevarthen, C., & Malloch, S. (2000). The dance of wellbeing: Defining the musical therapeutic effect. *Nordic Journal of Music Therapy*, *9*(2), 3–17. http://doi.org/10.1080/08098130009477996.

Trolldalen, G. (1997). Music therapy and interplay. A music therapy project with mothers and children elucidated through the concept of "appreciative recognition". *Nordic Journal of Music Therapy*, *6*(1), 14–27. https://doi.org/10.1080/08098139709477890.

Trondalen, G. (2005). 'Significant moments' in music therapy with young persons suffering from Anorexia Nervosa. *Music Therapy Today*, *VI*(3), 396–429.

Trondalen, G. (2009–2010). Exploring the rucksack of sadness: Focused, time-limited bonny method of guided imagery and music with a female executive. *Journal of Association for Music and Imagery*, *12*, 1–20.

Trondalen, G. (2016a). Musical relationship: An act of trust. In J. Strange, E. Richards, & H. Odell-Miller (Eds.), *Collaboration and assistance in music therapy practice. Roles, relationships, challenges* (pp. 9–12). London: Jessica Kingsley Publishers.

Trondalen, G. (2016b). Resource-oriented Bonny method og Guided Imagery and Music (R-oGIM) as a health resource for musicians. *Nordic Journal of Music Therapy*, *25*(1), 5–31. http://doi.org/10.1080/08098131.2014.987804.

Trondalen, G. (2016c). Self care in music therapy: The art of balancing. In J. Edwards (Ed.), Oxford Handbook of Music Therapy (pp. 936-956). Oxford: Oxford University Press.

Trondalen, G. (2019a). Musical intersubjectivity. *The Arts in Psychotherapy*, *65*, 101589. http://doi.org/10.1016/j.aip.2019.101589.

Trondalen, G. (2019b). GIM and life transitions: A relational perspective. In D. Grocke (Ed.), *Guided imagery and music: The Bonny method and beyond* (2nd ed., pp. 97–114). Dallas, TX: Barcelona Publishers.

Tronick, E. Z. (1998). Dyadically expanded states of consciousness and the process of therapeutic change. *Infant Mental Health Journal*, *19*(3), 290–299.

Tsiris, G. (2017). Music therapy and spirituality: An international survey of music therapists' perceptions. *Nordic Journal of Music Therapy*, *26*(4), 293–319. http://doi.org/10.1080./08098131.1239647.

UN. (2015). United nations, sustainable development goals, Agenda 2030. Retrieved from www.undp.org/sustainable-development-goals.

Valberg, T. (2011). *En relasjonell musikkestetikk. Barn på orkesterselskapenes konserter (A relational aesthetics of music–children at professional orchestras' concerts)* (Doctoral dissertation). Göteborg Universitet, Sweden.

van Manen, M. (1990). *Researching lived experience. Human science for an action sensitive pedagogy*. Western Ontario, London and Ontario, Canada: The State University of New York Press.

Various Artists. (2004). *Lullabies from the axis of evil*. Oslo: Kirkelig kulturverksted. Retrieved from https://kkv.no/musikk/utgivelser/2000-2009/2003/diverse-artister-4/.

Varkøy, Ø. (Ed.). (2012). *Om nytte og unytte (On utility and uselessness)*. Oslo: Abstrakt.

Westerlund, H., Karslen, S., & Kallio, A. (2021). Professional reflexivity and the paradox of freedom. Negotiating professional boundaries in a Jewish Ultra-Orthodox female music teacher education programme. *International Journal of Music Education*, *39*(4), 424–437. http://doi.org/10.1177/0255761421988924.

Whitehead-Pleaux, A., & Tan, X. (2016). *Cultural intersection in music therapy: Music, health, and the person*. Dallas, TX: Barcelona Publishers.

Williamon, A. (2004). *Music excellence. Strategies and techniques to enhance performance*. Oxford: Oxford University Press.

Winnicott, D. W. (1971). *Playing and reality*. London and New York: Tavistock/Routledge Publication.

Wittmann, M. (2017). *Felt time. The science of how we experience time* (E. Butler, Trans.). Cambridge, MA: MIT Press.

# Index

actions of martyrdom, music and 74
*aesthéticos* 9
aesthetics, Baumgarten 12
Agenda 2030 76
agential realism 23
Age of Enlightenment 11
Age of Reason 11
anorexia nervosa, video clip of 75–76
Antiquity 1, 4, 7, 24; Aristotle 11, 25; music in the 8; Plato 9–11; Pythagoras and Pythagoreans 8–9; Socrates 9–11
Apollonian 71, 72
*areté*, virtue 8, 10
Aristotle 11, 25
axis of evil 75

Barad, Karen 22, 23, 35, 42
Baumgarten, Alexander Gottlieb 12
body: carrier of subjectivity 64; lived 64; relationship and 64–66
Braidotti, Rosi 4, 49
Bruner, Jerome 62
Butler, Judith 66

calling, ethical musicality 70
capabilities 8, 76; combined 77, 78; concept of 76; creating 25, 39, 77; functionings 78; internal 77, 78; Nussbaum's theory on 16–17, 76–77; power of creating 25; Sen's approach 16; sustainability and hope 76–78
capacities 4, 68; ethical 20, 30, 65; human 61, 72; inborn 64, 77; innate 61; music 18, 39, 47, 61, 63; psycho-biological 60, 77; rational 12
Cassirer, Ernst 15
categorical imperative, Kant 12, 34
catharsis, music and 11
chronos, clock time 67
Civil Rights Movement, 'We shall overcome' 79–80
clock time 15, 67
Code of Ethics 38, 40
collaborative musicking 61–62, 72
communicative musicality 60–61; as human capacity 72; as ordinary 63
consensual model: embodied 20; emergent 20; intuitive 19–20; musical ethics 19–21; practice-oriented 20–21; relational 19
contemporary voices 4, 7, 24, 25; Higgins 18–19; Nussbaum 16–17; Phillips-Hutton and Nielsen 19–21; posthumanism lines of thought 21–24
COVID-19 pandemic 22; musician and audience 34; music performances during 44; music researcher 47
cultural immunogen 24

dark web, music for damage on 75
Declaration of Helsinki 48
difference 21
Dionysian 71
diversity 21; ethical musicality 70
doctrine of ethos 9; music 69

eating disorder 75–76
'eidein,' term 14
Elliot, David 30
*epistéme*, knowledge 10
epistemology of musicality 63
ethical awareness, musical therapist 41
ethical demand, Løgstrup 13
ethical dilemmas: lay musician 45; musical therapist 39–40; music educator 36–37; musician 34–35; musicologist 42–43; music researcher 47
ethical musicality 50–51; an art of becoming 81–82; body and relationship 64–66; concept of 59; conceptual framework 59, 83; context and involvement 69–73; embracing diversity 70; human ways of living 72–73; identity formation 71; music and ethics in lived 4; power and responsibility 73–76; reflexivity 59; sustainability and hope 76–81; time and space 67–69; *see also* musicality
ethical power of music, Pythagoras and Pythagoreans 8–9
ethical practices: 'lay' musician: ethics in everyday musicking 44–46; musical ethics relationship 30–31; music educator: ethics in teaching 35–38; musician: ethics in performance 32–35; musicologist: ethics in theory-building 41–44; music researcher: ethics in research 46–50; music therapist: ethics in therapy 38–41; real-music encounters 29, 50

ethical problems: lay musician 44–45; musical therapist 38–39; music educator 36; musician 33–34; musicologist 42; music researcher 47
ethico-onto-epistemology 23
ethics 1; core of 2; discipline 1, 2; everyday musicking by lay musician 44–46; music researcher 46–50; performance by musician 32–35; as practice in musical real-life settings 5; teaching by music educator 35–38; theory-building and musicologist 41–44; therapy by music therapist 38–41; virtue theory of 10, 11, 25
*eudaimonia*, human flourishing 8, 45
European Code of Conduct for Research Integrity 49

face of the Other 14, 71, 82
felt time 15
freedom 16; paradoxes of 76, 79

General Data Protection Regulations (GDPR) 47, 48, 75
Glaucon 10
Governance and Research Ethics Committees 48
Guided Imagery and Music (GIM) 68, 74

'Harmonia', metaphysical theory 8–9
health, sustainability and hope 76, 78–79
Higgins, Kathleen Marie 18–19
hope: music strategies creating 80–81; sustainability and 76–81
human beings: body and relationship 64–66; ethical musicality and ways of living 72–73; time and space 67–69
human dignity, principle of 48
human flourishing, *eudaimonia* 8, 45
human vulnerability, Nussbaum 16–17

# Index 93

identity, music contributing to 71
Indigenous music sustainability 80
information and communication technology (ICT) 78
informed consent, music researcher 48
intuitive ethics, concept of 19

*kátharsis* 11
kairos, subjective time 67
Kant, Immanuel 11–13
Kantianism 13
*katháros* 11
*Kirkelig Kulturverksted* record company 75
'kuchéza' 47

Langer, Susanne Katherina Knauth 14–16
language, music and 75
Law or a Code of Ethics 38
*Laws, The* (Plato) 10
lay musician, ethics in everyday musicking 44–46
Lévinas, Emmanuel 14, 35
lines of thought, posthumanism 21–24
listening, Guided Imagery and Music (GIM) 68, 74; music 67–69
lived ethics, research 76
lived experience 82; musical 3, 31, 64; musicality as 60–61, 63, 64; music and 15–16; music listening and 65–66; time and space 67–69
living ethics 73
Løgstrup, Knud Ejler Christian 13

Matherne, Samantha 13
mental offloading, engagement 20
mercy, Nussbaum on 17
modern philosophy 4, 7, 24, 25; Kant 11–13; Langer 14–16; Lévinas 14; Løgstrup 13
morality, values and 13
'mousiké' 8

music: access to 1–2; common arguments against 71–72; context of 2–3; dark web and damage 75; doctrine of ethos 69; ethical power of 8–9; ethical practices 29; globalization of 2; identity formation in 71; lived experience and 15–16; musical ethics relationship 30–31; musicking and 30; peace and conflict resolution 79–80; professionalization of 2; relational aesthetic of 31, 64–65; as social practice 31; spiritual experiences of 74; supporting destructive actions 74; technological developments 1–2; term 47; validation of 65
musical engagement 3
musical ethics: consensual model of Phillips-Hutton and Nilesen 19–21; as practice 5
musical-ethics-demand 50
musicality: communicative musicality 60–61; conception of 63; cultures of 60–63; epistemology of 63; lived experience 60; musicianship 60, 61–62; *see also* ethical musicality
*Music and Ethics* (Cobussen and Nielsen) 19
music asylum 69
music educator, ethics in teaching 35–38
musician: ethical queries 1; ethics in everyday musicking by lay 44–46; ethics in performance 32–35; instrument 32; music 32; music training of 33–35; performance 32–33; as person 33
musicianship 60, 61–62
musicking, music and 30
music listening 67–69
music of the spheres (*musica universalis*) 9
musicologist, ethics in theory-building 41–44

music-philosophical discourse 4; music and ethics 5; practical crossroads and 81, 82–83
music researcher, ethics in research 46–50
music therapist, ethics in therapy 38–41
*Music transforming conflicts* (Philips-Hutton) 80

*New Yorkers, The* (magazine) 17
Nielsen, Nanette, Phillips-Hutton and 19–21, 25
nomadic ethical subject 21
Nussbaum, Martha Craven 16–17

Other: ethical responsibility 50; face of the 14, 71, 82; improvisation 44; relational ethics 35
*Oxford Handbook of Western Music and Philosophy* (Tomlinson) 21

paradoxes of freedom 76, 79
Phillips-Hutton, Ariana: *Music transforming conflicts* 80; Nielsen and 19–21, 25
philosophy, Langer 14–16
*Philosophy in a New Key* (Langer) 15
phronesis, wisdom 10
plagiarism, music researcher 48–49
Plato 25; Socrates and 9–11
play 16–17
posthumanism, lines of thought 21–24
power, responsibility and in ethical musicality 73–76
proto-conversation, term 60
Pythagoras of Samos 8
Pythagoreans, power of music 9

reflexivity 59
relational aesthetic of music 31
relational ethics 35; Lévinas 14; Løgstrup 13
*Republic, The* (Plato) 10

research: ethics by music researcher 46–50; lived ethics 76; power and responsibility 75–76
research integrity, music researcher 49
responsibility, power and in ethical musicality 73–76
rhizome, term 23
Rostropóvich, Mstislav 79

scientific misconduct, music researcher 48–49
Sen, Amartya 16
slow music therapy 68
slow sociology 68
social nature, ethics of music 18
social practice, music as 31
Socrates, Plato and 9–11
South Africa, national anthem 80
spirituality, music experiences 74
Springsteen, Bruce 79
Stern, Daniel 62
storytelling, music and 75
subjective experience, felt time 15
sustainability 72; capability 76–78; health 76, 78–79; hope and 76–81; Indigenous music 80; paradox of freedom 76, 79

techné 8
technology, ethical musicality 78
terror, music and 74
'The Wall' (Springsteen) 79
throat, voice processing instrument 66
time 15; chronos (clock) 67; kairos (subjective) 67; space and 67–69
timeframe 15
training: musical therapist 40–41; musicology 43–44; music professionals 46; music researcher 48
training programmes: music education 38; musicianship 35
Truth and Reconciliation Commission 80

universal norm (utilitarian) 13
University College 41, 42
unpleasant experiences: lay musician 45–46; musical therapist 40; music educator 37; musician 35; music researcher 47–48
UN Sustainable Developmental Goals 76
utilitarian 13, 72

Vancouver Recommendations 47, 48
'Venceremos' ('We shall overcome') 80

Vetlesen, Arne Johan 2
Vietnam Veterans Memorial, Washington 79
virtue, areté 8, 10
virtue theory of ethics 10, 25; Aristotle 11
voice processing, throat 66

*What is Ethics* (Vetlesen) 2
wisdom, phronesis 10
World War I 80

For Product Safety Concerns and Information please contact our EU representative GPSR@taylorandfrancis.com
Taylor & Francis Verlag GmbH, Kaufingerstraße 24, 80331 München, Germany

www.ingramcontent.com/pod-product-compliance
Lightning Source LLC
Chambersburg PA
CBHW061959220426
43662CB00011B/1745